EXPLORING JAPANESE BOOKS AND SCROLLS

EXPLORING JAPANESE BOOKS AND SCROLLS

COLIN FRANKLIN

OAK KNOLL PRESS

THE BRITISH LIBRARY

2005

This facsimile edition was published in 2005 by

Oak Knoll Press
310 Delaware Street, New Castle, Delaware, USA
www.oakknoll.com
&
The British Library
96 Euston Road, London, NW1 2DB, UK

ISBN: 1-58456-164-5 (Oak Knoll Press)
ISBN: 0-7123-4910-3 (The British Library)

This work was originally printed as a fine press book in a larger format by
The Book Club of California in 1999. See colophon - page 157.

Title: Exploring Japanese Books and Scrolls
Author: Colin Franklin
Dust Jacket Design: Geoffrey E. Matheson
Publishing Director: J. Lewis von Hoelle

The British CIP Record for this book is available from The British Library, London, UK

Library of Congress Cataloging-in-Publication Data:

Franklin, Colin.
        Exploring Japanese Books and Scrolls / Colin Franklin.
               p. cm.
        Originally published: San Francisco, Calif. : Book Club of California, 1999.
        Includes Index.
        ISBN 1-58456-164-5
1. Illustrated books-Japan. 2. Scrolls, Japanese. I. Title.

Z1023.F83 2005
096'.1-dc22   2005047791

This work was printed and bound in China on archival, acid-free paper meeting the requirements
of the American Standard for Permanence of Paper for Printed Library Materials.

FOREWORD FOR THIS EDITION

Japanese books and scrolls continue to provide fascination, though the scene has greatly changed since I began collecting them thirty years ago. The bibliophile charm of Japan remains if strong temptations arrive they are not always resisted. One such temptation is mentioned on page 56, and it should in honesty be confessed that the strength of mind suggested there was short-lived. I am grateful to Robert Fleck, President of Oak Knoll Press, for his initiative in publishing a new edition of this book, and to his publishing colleague John von Hoelle for scrupulously looking after its production.

I was given the duty many years ago of going once a week to the Kegan Paul bookshop, opposite the British Museum, owned by the publishing firm where I worked, to 'check the books' – i.e., the accounts. No job could ever have been given to anyone less competent. Kegan Paul, Trench, Trubner called themselves "Specialists in Oriental and African Books' – a large specialization indeed. After whizzing through those pages of accounts and signing something or other, time was better spent viewing a few interesting oriental arrivals. In those scrupulous days it would not have been reckoned proper for me to have bought from the firm, with which I was associated. However, a seed was sown. I am grateful to the memory of Mr. Coles, the manager of Kegan Paul at that time, and for the very present friendship of Robert Sawers, enjoyably independent during more than three decades, who succeeded him. They were my first tutors, before journeys to Japan rose above the horizon.

For fuller treatment of these themes I suggest readers should consult any of Jack Hillier's excellent books, especially his final masterpiece in two large volumes, The Illustrated Books of Japan (Sotheby's publications, 1987); and a recent work of academic thoroughness by Peter Kornicki, The Book in Japan: A Cultural History from the Beginnings to the Nineteenth Century (Brill, 1998).

Colin Franklin
Culham, June 2005

ACKNOWLEDGEMENT

I AM most grateful to The Book Club of California for the friendly and generous spirit which has prevailed through this book's production; to Joanne Sonnichsen who encouraged me, over a pleasant luncheon in Amsterdam, to offer it to The Book Club of which she was then President; to Jonathan Clark who has taken immense care in its design and printing; and on my side of the Atlantic to Michael Dudley whose skill was responsible for excellent photography, at the Ashmolean Museum in Oxford, from examples in my collection. Those winter sessions, after hazardous handling of delicate objects, became agreeable social occasions.

As I have travelled to Japan about twenty-five times during as many years, this book has taken longer to prepare than others I have written, and no doubt it contains more blunders. I would not have attempted it without the friendship across four decades of Bob Sawers, connoisseur and enthusiast. My wife Charlotte, as ever, shared the quest and its pleasures—as has our son Gideon, especially when we were able to spend time together in Japan.

Colin Franklin
Culham, July 1999

TABLE OF CONTENTS

LIST OF ILLUSTRATIONS   PAGE   viii

INTRODUCTION: THE MILLION CHARMS   3

1   EARLY PRINTING   9

2   MANUSCRIPT EXAMPLES   23

3   PAINTED BOOKS I   31

4   PAINTED BOOKS II   41

5   ILLUSTRATED BOOKS I   53

6   ILLUSTRATED BOOKS II   69

7   ILLUSTRATED BOOKS III   89

8   SOME PHRASE-BOOKS FROM OLD JAPAN   101

9   MEISHO-ZUE   109

10 POSTSCRIPT ON MAPS   141

INDEX   151

LIST OF ILLUSTRATIONS

PLATE   PAGE

Philosopher with boy playing the *sho* (v. *page 50*) . . *Frontispiece*

1   *Hyakumanto* pagoda 2

2   *Hyakumanto* text 6-7

3   Block-printed images of Amida 11

4   Block-print with Amida ("smudged, with ink stains. . .") . 12

5   Woodcut opening of the Kofuku-ji scroll, Nara, 1383 . . 14-15

6   *Saga-bon:* Cover of a *Noh* play 16

7   Opening of the gold-on-blue Jingo-ji sutra . . . 24-25

8   Colophon of a Nara-period scroll 26

9   Opening of the gold-on-blue Nikko sutra . . . 27

10   Inside cover and opening of a *Noh* manuscript, early Edo period . 28-29

11   Cover, *Bun-sho Monogatari* (*Nara-chou*) . . . 33

12   From the *Bun-sho Monogatari* (early blue covers) . . 34

13   From the *Shotoku-Taishi Nara-ehon*, Volume I . . 36

14   From the *Shotoku-Taishi Nara-ehon*, Volume III . . 37

15   From the *Shotoku-Taishi Nara-ehon*, Volume IV . . 38

16   Scene of peace from the Kyoto *Nara-ehon* . . . 39

17   From the large album of paintings and calligraphy (section) . 40

18   Battle scene in the mysterious "California" scroll . . 42

19   In the kitchen, *Iwaya Monogatari* 43

20   Section of the Nara-ehon scroll, *Iwaya Monogatari* . . 43

21   Saintly trial before triumph, from the *Kitano-Tsuya Monogatari* . 44-45

22	Peace and scholarship, *Kitano-Tsuya Monogatari*	46
23	Calligraphy over fruit decoration on silk, *Kitano-Tsuya Monogatari*	46
24	A float in the procession, Gion Shrine	47
25	Entrance to the ceremonial procession, Gion Shrine	48-49
26	Opposing pages from the large album of paintings and calligraphy	50
27	Marrow fruit and flowers, from nine volumes of flower paintings	51
28	Section of a scroll on silk by Masuyama Sessai, with his signature	52
29	Lan T'ing Pavilion	55
30	Artist and banana leaf, from *Hasshu Gafu*	56
31	Poet and fir tree, from *Hasshu Gafu*	57
32	Bird and hops, from *Hasshu Gafu*	58
33	Bird and plums, from *The Mustard Seed Garden*	59
34	From *The Mustard Seed Garden*	59
35	Snow on blossom, from *The Mustard Seed Garden*	59
36	From *The Mustard Seed Garden*, 1756	60
37	From *The Mustard Seed Garden*, 1756	61
38	Lotus bud, from Morikuni's *Umpitsu Soga*	62
39	Kanyosai: Rabbits, from *Mokyo Wakan Zatsuga*	64-65
40	Kanyosai: Snail, from *Mokyo Wakan Zatsuga*	66
41	Bamboo, from *Ransai Gafu*, Volume I	67
42	Soken: from *Soken Sansui Gafu*, 1818. "In the bleak midwinter."	68
43	Soken: Calling them in to the restaurant, from *Yamato Jimbutsu Gafu*, II, 1804	70
44	Kiho: Domestic business, from *Kafuku Nimpitsu*	71
45	Minwa: Domestic bath, from *Manga Hyaku-jo*, 1814	71
46	From *Nantei Gafu*, 1804. "Relative peace in the kitchen."	72
47	Chinnen: from *Azuma No Teburi*, 1829. Domestic scene	73
48	From an album of paintings on silk by Taizan, circa 1790	74
49	Kunisada's parody of *Genji*: covers, wrapper and box	75
50	From Kunisada's parody of *Genji*	76-77

51 *Bumpo Gafu*, 1st series: "Rising like a graph of summer . . ." . 78

52 Bumpo, *Kanga Shinan Nihen*: Waterfall study . . . 78

53 *Kiho Gafu*, 1827: Reading, while he binds a sheaf . . . 79

54 From *Koshu Gafu*, 1812: The potter at his wheel . . 79

55 From *Taigado Gafo*: The poet in his pavilion . . 80

56 Double page from *Meika Gafu*, 1814 . . 80

57 From Chinnen, *Sonan Gafu*, 1834: Girl calligrapher . . 81

58 Hoitsu: from *Oson Gafu*, 1817 82-83

59 Masayoshi: from *Sansui Ryakuga-Shiki*, 1800 . . 84

60 Taniguchi Gesso: from *Haikai Hyaku Gasan*, 1816 . . 86

61 Large Shijo *Surimono* 87

62 Large Shijo *Surimono* 88

63 Hokusai: frontispiece to the "Thirty-six Immortal Women Poets" 91

64 Eishi: from the "Thirty-six Immortal Women Poets," 1801 . 92-93

65 From Utamaro's Insect Book, 1788: Frogs and lotus leaf . . 94

66 From Utamaro's "Picture Book of the Green Houses," 1804 . 95

67 Hokusai: "Hundred Views of Fuji." First issue covers . . 97

68 From Hokusai's "Hundred Views." Myth and myth below Fuji . 97

69 From Hokusai's "Hundred Views" 98

70 Furutani Korin: from album of bamboo designs, 1905 . . 98

71 From Kamisaka Sekka, *Momoyogusa*, 1909 . . . 99

72 From Kamisaka Sekka, *Momoyogusa*, 1909 . . . 100

73 *Kaei Tsugo*, 1855: "He forged a bill. . ." . . . 103

74 *Eigaku Kyoju*, 1873: "Italic Small Lotters" . . . 106

75 *Miyako Meisho Zue*: Shrine, Kyoto . . . 110

76 *Miyako Meisho Zue*: Making sake from rice . . . 111

77 *Miyako Meisho Zue*: Making and selling fans . . . 112

78 *Miyako Meisho Zue*: A merry picnic . . . 114-115

79 *Miyako Meisho Zue*: Restaurant by the river, Kyoto . . 116

80 *Miyako Meisho Zue*: Shopping street on the hill overlooking Kyoto 117

81 *Miyako Meisho Zue*: Admiring the blossom 117

82 *Miyako Meisho Zue*: Elegance in Kyoto . . . 118-119

83 *Miyako Meisho Zue*: Trouble in a high wind . . . 120

84 *Miyako Meisho Zue*: Cutting melons on a hot day . . . 121

85 *Miyako Meisho Zue*: The sweet shop, Kyoto . . . 121

86 *Edo Meisho Zue*: Tokyo in the late Edo period . . 122-123

87 *Edo Meisho Zue*: The publisher's shop, Edo . . . 124

88 *Nikko San Shi*: Mountain and waterfall . . . 125

89 From *Hanshin Meisho Zue*, 1916 127

90 "Castaway" manuscript: The balloon ascent . . 132-133

91 "Castaway" manuscript: Skyscrapers . . . 135

92 Nagakubo Sekisui: World Map, 1785 . . . 142-143

93 Shiba Kokan: World Map, 1792 146-147

EXPLORING JAPANESE BOOKS AND SCROLLS

Plate 1. Hyakumanto *pagoda*

THE MILLION CHARMS

Some explanation is needed for daring to touch this subject. So many books and exhibition catalogues exist for reference, with generous rations of well-printed illustrations in color, and essays or chapters of introduction, that it would be absurd if I were to dip a toe into the edge of such an abundant spring. I could not pretend to approach the scholarship of their authors. Yet still there remains apparent difficulty and mystery about the subject. Few visitors to the exhibitions understand Japanese, or approach the calligraphy with any comprehension. The most lucid essays have a lot of transliterated names and titles which do not linger in most memories—like this:

> Indeed, only one *Hiei-zan-ban* is known, the one-hundred-and-fifty-*maki* version of the *Hokke sandaibu* with attendant commentaries. In all, this consisted of three of the principal works of Tendai Buddhism, the *Hokke-gengi* (twenty *maki*), the *Hokke mongu* (twenty *maki*) and the *Makashikan* (twenty *maki*), with three important commentaries on these works, the *Hokke-gengi-shakusen* (twenty *maki*), the *Hokke mongu-ki* (thirty *maki*) and the *Makashikan bugyo-Koketsu* (forty *maki*). This vast printing enterprise took eighteen years to complete, from 1278 to 1296. Unfortunately, very few complete copies survive.[1]

Or this, on the ever-popular subject of papermaking:

> For paper, *torinoko* and *doromaniai* were used. *Torinoko* is a smooth, faintly yellow paper resembling the shell of a chicken's egg. In former times it was made of *gampi* (*Wikstroemia gampi*) and the paper mulberry, but now *mitsumata* (*Edgeworthia papyrifera*) is used. There are three grades: thin, medium, and thick. They serve for such purposes as bonds and official documents.[2]

These random examples, child's-play for members of the club, are quoted only to show that outsiders—most of us—will not find such chapters a riveting read. They may be, as the phrase goes, counter-productive in pasting a large notice above this subject, with a warning: "*Keep Off. These Matters are Difficult.*" The truth is they are also delightful, and may be approached by different routes. Such is the excuse for my attempt.

Brainless in facts of political history, which enter as I read and depart without trace, I have lived under privilege by visiting Japan about twenty-five times as a bookseller during the last twenty years. These journeys included blissful holiday sometimes, in the southern islands of Shikoku and Kyushu, north in Hokkaido, more remotely on Oki Island towards Korea, and in Amami Oshima where silk-weaving for kimonos is still a cottage industry. With Japanese friends I have travelled to watch the paper-makers in distant villages, and heard their work-songs. More relevant to this essay, it seemed to me during my first visit foolish to be concerned only with introducing Western books to Japan—that I should be interested equally in learning about their books.

The thought sank home, penetrating my slow responses, some years later when a Japanese friend in Tokyo took us to visit a major exhibition of calligraphy which spread through several great rooms of the Tokyo National Museum in Ueno Park. There we viewed Buddhist texts in contrasting hands upon a variety of papers and on silk; hanging scrolls of thick brush-characters, poems we were told, done by priests or princes in drunken sessions of the night; long scrolls or *maki-mono* partly opened, perhaps showing household accounts or tax returns, of eloquent elegance.

Maki-mono means scroll, and so a few Japanese terms slowly arrive, making better sense of a paragraph quoted above, taking up residence. But the memorable moment for me was in leaving that exhibition, which had been crowded through all its huge area. "It must be marvellous for Japanese people," I said, a silly commonplace, "to be able to read all these things." "Not at all," was the reply; "I don't suppose one person in a hundred can read them." And the penny dropped. If they can so greatly enjoy this visually, it struck me, cannot I share that appreciation to some small extent, just by looking? So began the seed of a collecting idea.

A hint had presented itself during my first visit to Japan, in 1973. The occasion was an international "congress" for booksellers, and book fair. Congress means feasts, jaunts, dreary lectures and disparate exhibitions. At these, one noticed that the opening exhibit time and again was a small wooden pagoda [Plates 1–2] with a top which pulled off like the stopper of a medicine bottle, to expose a hollow housing a small printed scroll (or *maki-mono*). These little paper scrolls, Buddhist incantations or "charms," were known in four kinds, four different texts. The point of high fascination was that they could be dated with some precision to the year 770 A.D.—interest rising to excitement upon finding, at the fair, that several Japanese booksellers also exhibited the pagodas with their printed scrolls, for sale.

It seemed extraordinary that anybody could buy, without fearful extravagance, an object of such veneration and antiquity. I chose two, for as soon as it became known that one was sold to me, a Californian bookseller revealed that he owned another, which I could have for even less. Idiotically, those two I sold again in Japan some years later in the ordinary life of bookselling but have replaced them since, less wisely, with a faultless example which is here to stay. In these and other forms of Japanese collecting one must beware of forgery—but that tiresome episode is for a later chapter.

The pagodas with their scrolls, about two feet long when spread, are known as *Hyakumanto Darani*, "a million charms." The ruling Empress Shotoku, a formidable and devious character, learning about the new technique of woodblock printing which was practiced in China, gave orders for a million of these to be made and stored in ten Buddhist temple treasuries. It is believed that a million were indeed made, a prodigious work of carving, papermaking and printing.

Buddhists achieved grace, it was thought, through many kinds of repetition and reproduction. To say the name of Buddha, to carve his image, visualize it, paint or print it, helped. As repetition was a merit, printing offered special opportunities. Sutras— defined as "sacred texts believed to preserve the actual words of the historical Buddha," the Indian prince Siddhartha Gautama [563–483 B.C.]—were written as a major industry in the many temples. The image of Buddha was printed in multiple small impressions like sheets of stamps; making them formed an act of grace. Similarly, to a less extent, visitors to the temples acquired grace by buying them, the more impressions the better, according to what they could afford, and that suited everyone.

The little pagodas ordered by the Empress were her own salvation, not for sale. It is astonishing that to this day hundreds of them survive in one of the temples, the Horyu-ji in Ikaruga, near Nara, which originally received them. There one views the assembly behind a glass wall, a few larger than the rest to mark each ten-thousand completed, several giants recording each hundred-thousand.

Their existence in the 1973 book fair was not inexplicable; their creation had witnessed the advent of Buddhism in Japan, their sale its decline. Survival was

訶 燒 薩 㗬 伐 吽 婆 十 九 摩 薩 麗 剌 揭 六
引 達 婆 嚩 羅 引 盧 薩 跋 塞 婆 眤 尼 多 薩
尼 播 毗 擎 薩 褐 婆 羅 訖 愻 末 七 摩 毗 婆
莎 波 泥 㗧 漿 尼 薩 跋 㮈 伱 麗 毗 廋 怛 達
引 毗 二十 毗 尼 一十 墀 囉 帝 南 八 布 摟 地

perhaps in the luck of an island, for Japan, like Britain and Venice, had as islands generally been spared such a history of invasion as made Korean antiquities, for instance, far more rare. Civil wars, many fires, and earthquakes caused chronic destruction, but Japan had cherished a policy of isolation and through more than twelve centuries those pagodas have remained at the Horyu-ji temple.

In 1868, just over a century before my first visit, the Emperor Meiji changed that traditional isolation to acceptance of both travellers and travel, sanctioning the import of such varied blessings as Christianity, science and industry. The first of those three had enjoyed periods of high success in Japan already, balanced by times of appalling persecution. Beside swamps of boiling mud in Shikoku are notices recording the death by torture of Jesuits in that place. But at the Meiji restoration Christianity became fashionable, along with Western clothes and art; correspondingly Buddhism went into partial eclipse, lacked funds to keep its temples in order, and redressed the balance by selling a few of its accumulated treasures. Thus Eastern art-collecting became possible in Europe, and the *Hyakumanto Darani* found their way to that book fair in Tokyo. Nobody knows just how many were sold by the temple in Nara, before such peccadillos became illegal, but it was as if some private press had issued a small edition in the late nineteenth century, in rather larger numbers than those of the Kelmscott Press. Nobody would expect them to have become impossibly rare a hundred years later.

That gives a reasonable perspective for certain Japanese artifacts in collections; I have in mind books and scrolls, but it would also apply in varying degrees to sculpture, for example, and to pots and paintings. The printed texts stored in small pagodas seem to offer an ideal start to any Japanese collection, as was apparent in those public exhibitions where we saw them—and by their adoption as emblem of the Antiquarian Booksellers' Association of Japan. For they provide three points of fundamental interest: antiquity, paper, and the earliest surviving examples of printing in the world.

Such claims need, as ever, qualification and hesitation. Antiquity is not in doubt, but paper had been used in China since the third century and a knowledge of printing (as of Buddhism) also came to Japan from China. The little printed scrolls, and growing mass of lengthy manuscript scrolls, were written in Chinese by priests and scholars for the very few, Japanese being then a spoken language without alphabet or syllabary. The writing of scrolls, like those printed charms, was an act of grace. If more books are published than read in twentieth-century Europe—hardly an act of grace—more sutras were written than used in eighth-century Japan. Until lately it was possible to find them, remarkable and beautiful survivors.

All this, in comparison with European books, has been a surprising field to explore. How in England is one to discover, outside such places as the Bodleian or British Library, complete eighth-century manuscripts? Printing came West many centuries later, and paper was first seen there in twelfth-century Italy.

The Japanese never used parchment; they knew the quality of their paper, which therefore had a higher artistic presence than it achieved in Europe. Large supplies were needed, even in those early years; one complete sutra could extend to more than six hundred scrolls, or *maki*, and the average length of one scroll was perhaps seven written yards. Temples may still possess entire sutras from that period; private collectors make do with single scrolls.

Paper remains a wonderful and excessive subject in Japan. To have a notion of its place as art one should read at random a few chapters in *The Tale of Genji*, where Prince Genji is forever showing his sensibility by choosing with exquisite propriety the shade and texture for poems or notes to his paramours. Paper and calligraphy alike bring gasps of appreciation from the recipients, envy from their attendants, the perfection of the prince's style detectable instantly.

I find it an equivocal subject; admiring the colors, textures, patterns, knowing the unpleasant conditions of work for those who make it. English handmade paper is hard to find now, only one or two places producing it in any quantity; the quality is excellent, different entirely from mould-made paper (next best thing) or machine-made; but there exists no tradition comparable with the Japanese where papers differed for each occasion and purpose: sutras at one pure extreme, toys and shop-wrapping at another, all attractive and appropriate in their degree. Every few years some large and expensive book is published, in a limited edition with mounted samples, declaring that the number of workshops producing such papers is so drastically declining that it will not be possible to produce such a volume again, and yet they appear.

Paper was made from vegetable fiber, the bark of certain trees, stripped and pulped and pulverized. It is still possible to see everything done as for those early sutras, but nobody would envy the women whose arms swell blue from daily work in the cold-water vats, sifting slimy pulp for impurities. Though modern methods earn qualified regret, it was astonishing to arrive one bright morning at a farm where papermaking occupied the winter and agriculture the summer. We were late, and they could not afford to lose sunlight by waiting. Walking up wide steps to the yard we seemed to view a semicircle of surfboards tilted to the sun, each with its long strip of new paper, made that day and drying out. The papermakers needed to complete a large order from an American scholar in Japan, who had commendably taken up sutra-writing.

The aesthetic nuances of Japanese paper and calligraphy were never limited to Buddhist life in temples, though that was where and why they first flourished. Empresses were important in early Japanese history; we have encountered the Empress Shotoku, who ordered the little pagodas and their printed "charms." Another, the Empress Komyo, a generation earlier mourned the death of her husband in a practical and sympathetic way for which we must be deeply grateful, handing over all physical details of his life to the great Todai-ji in Nara for eternal preservation. That archive contained of course his treasures, works of art, bowls, musical instruments, but equally it included receipts, accounts, rice bags, measures, lengths of cloth, games, the apparatus of an Emperor's home and work twelve centuries ago. By amazing chance it survives, a private collection, only available to public view for two weeks each November in Nara, when the keeper of that Treasury (the Shoso-in) chooses a few very varied objects for exhibition. By good fortune I have twice been in Nara when such a display was there, the elaborate and the humblest shown together. The daughter-in-law of that Empress who cared so movingly about her husband's death as to preserve his inanimate life, had aimed for immortality in cherishing her own. A small witness of it exists in a wooden pagoda, still partly covered with crushed-oyster pigment, and the printed scroll it contained which is flattened now in a frame.

1. Chibbett, David, *The History of Japanese Printing and Book Illustration*, p.52
2. Shimizu, Yutaka, *Nara Picture Books*, translated by Richard Zumwinkle, 1960

CHAPTER ONE
EARLY PRINTING

Sir George Sansom, high in the tradition of British scholar-diplomats, declared that Japanese was a language perfectly suited to such a brief alphabet as the West invented; that its misfortune was to be burdened with the Chinese syllabary of many thousands of characters, or adaptations and reductions of it. The great adaptation was a running hand known as *kana* (devised in the ninth century by the genius of Koyasan, Kobo Daishi), which came into use during the early Fujiwara period.

As to these "periods" and their subdivision, early dates are simple: the city of Nara with its array of temples, planned upon the grid-model of a Chinese town, was founded in 710; the brief Nara period ended before that century closed, in 794, when the court escaped from a threat of Buddhist dominance to found its new capital at Heian-Kyo, present-day Kyoto. So began the Heian period, which lasted four centuries until 1185 but is commonly split as Early Heian (the first hundred years) and Late Heian. For roughly three centuries, Late Heian period, Japan was controlled by the Fujiwara family. Under its influence an aesthetic fastidiousness prevailed, familiar from such paintings and sculpture as survive and from many episodes in the Lady Murasaki's *The Tale of Genji*, which is accepted as a portrait of courtly elegance and intrigue among the Fujiwara clan.

She could never have written it without the advent of *kana* script, the running hand. Chinese characters, called *kanji*, were still used for sutras and formal purposes;

kana made possible a spate of literature from brief poems to correspondence and epic. There seems sometimes to be no clear equivalent in English for artistic concepts from the Japanese. As fluent repartee, so common in *Genji*, exchanged messages possess precision of syllabic brevity but carry small suggestion of wit or poetry even in Arthur Waley's translation. Yet the elegance of response, of formal emotion upon perfect paper, is there; very early manuscripts of that long text exist, beautifully written in the running hand which these days is known as *hiragana*.

One fact in the history of books is that any form of Chinese or Japanese had far too many characters to be managed with any ease in movable type; another to perplex us is the prior invention, in the second decade of the fifteenth century, of printing by movable type in Korea and its early use a century later in Japan. But it was not the appropriate way, and despite a few rare (occasionally superb) surviving examples the proper method was woodblock. The development of printing in Japan is a history of block books. The use of movable type there is perhaps comparable with the use of block books in Europe.

And that is how printing continued, until a late introduction of lithography and photography in the last quarter of the nineteenth century. As so often happens when widespread skills exist, woodblock printing continued long after new techniques reduced its need. Like rice cultivation, it was and is an aspect of the Japanese way of life.

Enough hardwood grew in Japan to provide blocks for all the needs of printing and sculpture. As with any block-printing in the West, where both wood and metal were used, a block (unlike type) could only hold one text, which endured for indefinite reprinting in new editions. Thus Japanese printed books have all the complexity and nuance familiar to print collectors in Europe. The matter is conveniently ignored, an uncharted continent. One is dependent upon the experienced eyes of a connoisseur, a quick assumption of private taste and flair ("never trust experts"), the persuasive charm of booksellers (possession bends judgement)—or, with better but imperfect science, upon the character of paper. Blocks of course could be recut, but then the evidence becomes much simpler.

Japan's determined isolation resulted in a long-lived ignorance of printing from engraved metal plates. The first to practice it there was the heretical artist Shiba Kokan (1747–1818), who followed his anarchic spirit into several activities at the doubtful edge of law and custom, towards the close of the eighteenth century.

The woodcut artists advanced their skills to perfection, though in early centuries there was not much call for illustration of printed texts. The clearest authority on this was David Chibbett, in charge of the Japanese collection at the British Museum, who tragically died young after completing his *History of Japanese Printing and Book*

Illustration. Until the last decade of the sixteenth century, he wrote there, "no book was produced outside a temple and very few books not related to Buddhism were produced at all."[1] The second relevant fact is that "the earliest known example of native illustration in a printed book appeared in the second decade of the fifteenth century."[2] For about 650 years after the introduction of printing and knowledge of woodcut, therefore, no "native illustration" was attempted (or has survived); and it would be wrong to assume that much of the printing done in temples was illustrated; indeed, writes Chibbett again, "the earliest known fully authenticated example of a printed illustration specifically designed for a printed text"[3] was a conventional Buddhist frontispiece, such as will be familiar from manuscript scrolls, to a sutra produced in Ueno province in 1239.

So an interest in early Japanese printing confines itself to stamped repetitive Buddha images, conventional frontispieces (in the Kamakura period and after) for brief or longer Buddhist texts, and sutra scrolls, all produced in the temples.

It may therefore be less than astonishing to learn that this has remained a relatively neglected field of collecting in the West—which tends also

Plate 3. Block-printed images of Amida

to mean the East, because Japan wakes to its own excellence only after discovering it is desired abroad. The early printing was (with exceptions) not upon decorative or colored papers; nothing except geography connects it with the fashionable taste that sought Sharaku's actors, Utamaro's girls, Hokusai's waves, Hiroshige's Tokaido Road; no influence floated out towards *japonisme*; the Goncourt brothers never thought to desire it.

You may still see, framed on a bookshop wall or mounted as a hanging scroll, those multiple Buddha images like whole sheets of postage stamps printed any time from the twelfth to the sixteenth century [Plates 3 & 4]. "The peak in the development of the ancient print," wrote Mosaku Ishida in his excellent book[4] "came in the Kamakura period, when a vast number of stamped or printed Buddhas and pagodas were produced." The reference is to *printed* pagodas, within or beside which the Buddhas sometimes sat.

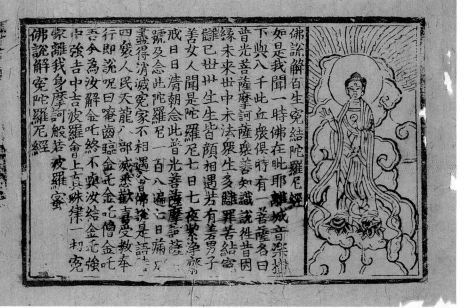

Plate 4. *Block-print with Amida ("smudged, with ink stains. . .")*

For themselves and for what they represented, these remain touching and surprising survivals. Two such sheets are beside me, the earlier example on thin paper (which must also be strong) with strands of its fiber structure prominent. It shows the Amida, seated on a lotus arranged like the base of an artichoke, and seems to be an early example—from the Late Heian period—similar to that illustrated on Page 102 of Mosaku Ishida's book and upon its jacket. I should quickly become lost in attempting to find my way among Buddhist deities, but Amida was a particularly sympathetic figure who appealed to the Fujiwara clan and all followers of Kobo Daishi—and is defined by Ishida as "Buddha of the Western Pure Land or Paradise, where he receives all who call upon his name." The notion of salvation through uttering the name of Amida, attractive because trouble-free, lent itself especially to the printing of such multiple images. The example illustrated in Ishida was found inside a seated statue of Amida and is described as "National Treasure"—but that was thirty years ago, and new discoveries occur inside such statues from time to time. Placing a hoard of them thus, before erecting and completing the sculpture, extends our concept of the merit which they conveyed.

The other sheet represents a fierce *fudo* or manifestation of the Buddhist spirit; "a powerful conqueror of evil, he is shown in many frightening aspects." He squats, holds a weapon, is surrounded by flame, a very different presence from Amida. The paper is comparable but rather less thin. It would have been rare to find paper of different character used for the same purpose, for there was in such matters a strict sense of fitness.

Both sheets pre-date the earliest examples of woodblock printing—of any printing—in Europe. The overtones of their origin, their honesty and antiquity, make them entirely attractive as works of art. A central Shinto creed was and is that certain places possess divine mystery or presence; this may easily be believed of these.

Other kinds of early woodblock print remain accessible, viewable, available outside the common orbit of Western collection, but few were illustrated. Rare examples survive in temples and public collections, all cut in imitation of Chinese models, generally as a formal frontispiece to the printed work. Antiquity, paper, subject are there for appreciation; it is usual to say that they lack delicacy, are not there for any decorative reason—yet, that was often the response to fifteenth-century German woodcut illustration until William Morris pointed to its expressive vigor.[5]

Pre-Tokugawa illustrations to printed books are therefore few, uncommon, and copied from the Chinese (except for just one very beautiful work in the Japanese style produced at the end of the fourteenth century, and another at the end of the sixteenth). Approachable and surviving examples keep their quality of awe, surprising us by a conviction or assurance which may or may not bear trace of "artistic purposes." One such, placed asymmetrically on poor paper, the Buddha enthroned, head against the sun and feet on lotus flowers, occupies one quarter of a rectangle and points to columns of text which fill the rest of it [Plate 4]. Smudged, with ink stains in one margin—who will declare what is art or ornament? Somebody in a temple printed this, somebody visiting bought and kept it.

A well-charted example dates from 1383, an enormous and revered sutra of six hundred scrolls (*maki*, volumes) produced at the Kofuku-ji in Nara. Each volume opens with a woodcut frontispiece of the Buddha with attendant deities [Plate 5]. The small bald-headed pilgrim under a canopy is a great Chinese scholar, Hsuan-Tsang, who translated many Buddhist scriptures from Sanskrit. The deities are instructed to provide protection for his journey home. Cloud-forms above and below set this scene at a distance from common life. Thick lines do not reduce its eloquence; small scholar and large idea, fierceness of protection he needed in the world. Buff-dyed paper has kept its strength; each column of large Chinese characters is printed within silver borders. A wholly Japanese cloud-effect in silver and gold flake decorates—artistically—the covers.

Though borders between Japanese art and Chinese influence are sometimes indistinguishable—because Japan took often and eagerly from Chinese example—

nobody could question the surprise of one sudden Japanese arrival in the late fourteenth century, an edition of the *Yuzu-nembutsu-engi* in two long scrolls printed between 1390 and 1414, most delicately illustrated in the indigenous or Tosa style with long slender woodcuts, hand-colored. Sophistication had thus arrived; it had no growth in the history of Japanese printing during the next two centuries; yet this example existed.

There is no reason to forget or ignore the Chinese-influenced woodcuts which appeared from time to time before the Tokugawa revolution at the close of the sixteenth century. Their Buddhist character and temple origin did not remove them from familiar life. Eight editions are recorded, from the Kamakura to the Tokugawa period, of a charming series known as the "Ten Ox-Herding Pictures." The ox symbolizes one's true self; the woodcuts follow in sequence as the man seeks his ox, finds him, is pulled uphill, rides him blissfully, finally conquers and leaves the animal as he himself achieves contemplation. The focal moment as he rides the ox, in control and happily playing the flute, became a favorite subject for artists and may be encountered by itself in scroll-paintings out of series, a curious composition unless one can recognize the context.

But most early Japanese printing, plain text without illustration, from Buddhist temples of one sort or another across about five centuries before the Tokugawa period, has not been commonly collected or recognized in the West. Indeed it is not glamorous, with certain obvious exceptions which owe their beauty to the quality, variety and decoration of papers rather than the printing. How could it be otherwise? In Japan woodcutters possessed near-perfect skills of imitation, a tradition which continues to this day. They had every economic reason to cultivate it. Printing, which began there many centuries earlier than in Europe, depended upon that art; natural aspiration and temple piety combined to approach perfection. It was so at Mainz for Gutenberg's Bible, and among the printers who followed him; calligraphy was imitated so that printing would provide a similar experience

for readers. Innovation, other than technical, formed no part of any printer's ambition; it was the purest form of adventureless imitation.

Much attention is given, perhaps with excessive emphasis, to the advent of movable type in sixteenth-century Japan. Though not quite comparable with the issue of block-books in fifteenth-century Europe, it was an aberration, used across a short period and of no technical importance in the history of Japanese printing. New methods prove themselves by driving out the old, or at least co-existing, but this did neither. Sir George Sansom wrote that the Japanese language was well suited to some such system as our own alphabet, but it was and is saddled with a complex syllabary instead. Movable type had by its nature far too many characters to be found and moved by any sane compositor; block books were nature's method. Block-cutters in Japan, like punch-cutters in Europe, perfectly imitated the calligraphy of their moment. It remained the valid method for a thousand years.

So, why all the fuss about movable type in Japan? Mutual pleasure upon common ground explains much of it. Koreans are proud to be known as the pre-Gutenberg inventors of it, though woodblocks were more appropriate there also and their use continued. As movable type marked the beginning of printing and spread of culture in Europe (block-books having negligible influence except upon rich collectors), the period of its employment in Japan provides some mutual recognition across the great divide; but it has small cultural importance. If European histories contained fewer repetitions of the phrase, so also would the Japanese.

Two other facets of that brief period, about 1590 to 1650, have their place in the aesthetic and cultural history of Japan: the first was native Japanese, the second Portuguese Jesuit. Both arrived at almost the same moment, by chance, from quite different sources.

Travellers in Korea to this day may feel saddened by the havoc of the Japanese invasion four centuries ago under Toyotomi Hidayoshi. He was defeated and turned away, after causing vast damage which is still visible in Seoul and elsewhere. Remembered bitterly by the Koreans, he took back to Japan their clever knowledge of printing with movable wooden types. Hidayoshi became the patron of major works printed by this method in Japan, using an especially large bold form of *kanji* cast in metal, which was probably not in imitation of current calligraphy. His successor, Ieyasu, founder of the long-lasting Tokugawa government or *bakufu*, also favored the printing of large-scale Buddhist works by metal movable type. In the same period an aesthetic movement, which has been compared with that of the private presses in England, appeared in Edo (now Tokyo). A printer and an artist, Hon'ami Koetsu and Suminokura Soan, used wooden movable types for several major works including a long series of *Noh* plays [Plate 6]. They worked at Saga outside Kyoto; their books are known as *Saga-bon*. The calligraphy-as-woodcut is most elegant, even to ignorant alien eyes, but

Plate 6. Saga-bon: Cover of a Noh play

equally the pleasure of those books is in their paper, often decorated with background designs in mica-dust, and in the multi-colored covers similarly designed. Movable type happened to be fashionable at court, its use incidental rather than responsible.

The other facet of movable type in Japan is more comprehensible, brought by the Jesuits who, favored by Hidayoshi, were therefore favored by many thousands of

Japanese people, rapid "converts" to Christianity. The Jesuits printed in the way known to them, with metal movable type, on presses they brought from Portugal. As later waves of persecution made their books very rare, these have become most highly coveted by collectors in Japan and the West. Again, the detail that they printed from movable type is incidental but their books show a fascinating acquaintance with European printing in their use of printers' flowers, borders, and a roman font for phrases of the creed in Latin, explained at length in Japanese.

Mainstream Japanese printing from the Heian to Meiji periods (or earlier)—from the eighth century to the nineteenth—meant block-books, whole pages cut on wood. Storage of so much wood caused formidable problems, as did its growth and preparation. One major work often produced, the *Daihannya-kyo Sutra* ("Sermons and Sayings of the Buddha") ran to six hundred long scrolls or volumes. The destruction of temples where these were printed, by fire or war, was not uncommon.

One landmark in the history of Japanese literature, and to a smaller extent of Japanese printing, was the invention by one of the Buddhist sects, in the ninth century, of a truly Japanese syllabary. Before, there was only Chinese, which could be used in two ways: as Chinese, the learned language—like Latin in the West—or as Japanese, using the Chinese syllabary to pronounce (syllable by syllable) Japanese words. There had been no written Japanese, except by employing this awkward method—which would only have been available to priests and a very few others equipped to read Chinese.

To the founder of Shingon Buddhism, a monk called Kobo Daishi, is attributed the invention of a syllabary for the Japanese language, the running hand still in common use, the form of *kana* called *hiragana*. The effect upon secular writing in Japan was very great, allowing educated men and women at court to correspond and write books. The Lady Murasaki in the tenth century was able to write her enormous novel, already mentioned, *The Tale of Genji*, because *hiragana* existed as a tool for her use. Upon printing the effect was less than one might have expected, because very few secular books circulated except in manuscript before the Tokugawa period and all printing was done by priests in the temples until 1590. It had its effect, however, because Zen Buddhism appealed more widely, to a greater social distance, than earlier forms, and some books were produced by Zen temples in the *hiragana* script.

For all the reasons lightly mentioned above—the late and incidental use of movable type, extreme rarity of any illustration in printed books, and limitation of printing to Buddhist works produced in temples—one is left to choose between a large ignorance of early Japanese printing, or the brash decision to view and understand a little of these temple editions and their variations, within the ordinary limits of inability to comprehend—encouraged by the memory of those crowds at the Tokyo National Museum, who viewed with fascination the old calligraphy they could not read.

There is no need for close acquaintance with the history of Japan to follow a rough geography of temple printing. Two internal wars punctuated it, the first establishing the Kamakura period, the second opening the Tokugawa or Edo period which lasted for three centuries. The earlier, mid-twelfth century war—subject of a classic epic, the *Heike Monogatari*—ended an era of rule by the Fujiwara family during which artistic appreciation had thrived (as it always did through the history of Japan, but that was a time of official or courtly encouragement). The Taira and Minamoto clans had their great struggle, in which the Minamoto chief Yoritomo was victorious. He moved the centre of power to Kamakura and founded there a form of military government, quite separated from the emperor who remained near Kyoto, called the *bakufu*; and this became the system of rule until the Meiji revolution (always called "restoration") in the third quarter of the nineteenth century.

The attention of these few pages has been upon the period *entre deux guerres*, Eliot's phrase in another context, from the Kamakura period to that second war which opened two and a half centuries (1615–1867) of Tokugawa rule. Different Buddhist sects had arrived much earlier from China, in the Nara and Heian periods, but very few examples of printing survive from that time. As printing was confined to Buddhist temple sources, the four main streams of Buddhism in Japan become relevant. The places where these Buddhist works were printed followed the spread of those sects, in Nara, Kyoto and elsewhere. Some of the most beautiful early printing was done in Nara, because the Fujiwara family in late Heian times had connections with particular temples there. The Kyoto neighborhood is remembered for greater variety of publications, but with less opulent patronage.

The four sects of Buddhism look confusing if one mentions that the first of the four was really six, all of them in Nara. These six divisions of Mahayana Buddhism at Nara included several of the largest and finest temples which—much burnt and rebuilt—are visited with admiration to this day, as for example the Todai-ji, the Kofuku-ji, and the Horyu-ji where one still sees those surviving small pagodas with their scrolls, the *Hyakumanto Darani* from the eighth century. These and other temples represented the six Mahayana sects, and with special connections to the Fujiwaras some produced sutras of great refinement on strong smooth paper flecked with silver and gold. Books printed at Kofuku-ji in this way were dedicated at the Shinto shrine of Kasuga, a form of Fujiwara piety which demonstrates the mutual absorption or co-existence of Buddhist and Shinto traditions. These *Kasuga-ban* books, prepared with much elegance in the thirteenth century after the high period of Fujiwara power, survive in a few collections and are much coveted.

Kyoto printing, more diffuse and not recognizable in any simple way, included the two "esoteric" sects of Mahayana Buddhism which were not far from each other in spirit and rank together as one—as the second of these four Buddhist divisions. Both were brought to Japan from China at the beginning of the ninth century; Dengyo Daishi established the Tendai sect at Hiei-zan near Kyoto, and Kobo Daishi (mentioned already as inventor of the *hiragana* script) founded the Shingon sect at Koyasan in the mountains further away. Despite the geographic distance, printing at both places ranked as Kyoto-based, or *Kyoraku-han*. Both places produced printed works, known as *Hieizan-ban* and *Koya-ban*; printings from the thirteenth century survive in a few collections.

Both kinds of Buddhism keep a large following in modern Japan. Tendai has its university with a fine and famous library; Koyasan, which keeps its isolation, is a deeply impressive place of pilgrimage reached by winding roads into the hills or a hot walk from the train. A cold night in one of its temple hostels leaves a memory of isolation and mountain air. Tall cryptomeria trees form a forest half-hiding the thousands of graves and memorials of those who are recorded there. The chief priest of the sect receives each year from the Emperor new vestments of pink silk brocade patterned with his imperial emblem; old pieces of this material are used as

scroll-mounts at Koyasan. Kobo Daishi is revered as a living presence. After seeing his tomb in the forest I asked foolishly when he died. "Well," I was told with embarrassment, "you see, we do not think he died." Clothes are still provided for him, food and water placed there each day.

The third and fourth sects of Buddhism to arrive in Japan were called Jodo ("Pure Land") and Zen. Pure Land doctrine, ascribed to a priest called Honen Shonin, became popular in thirteenth-century Japan, having been introduced at the end of the twelfth. Its popularity among the less perfectly educated is not hard to understand, for they had only to view an image of Amida, or say the name of that deity, to acquire grace. With such a wide circle of pious friends, it is not surprising that statues of Amida always appear calm and at peace. A broadside woodcut portrait of Honen Shonin survives, made in 1315 just over a century after his death. Pure Land has particular importance in the history of printing, for having produced in 1365 the first work in *hiragana* script—reflecting thus the more widespread following enjoyed by this sect. A single volume from 1259 formerly in the Hyde collection shows a more elevated or luxurious form of Pure Land printing (*Jodokyo-ban*), with large clear *kanji* on mica-sprinkled paper.

The fourth sect, brought to Japan from China by a priest called Eisai in the twelfth century and his pupil Dogen in the thirteenth, was Zen, which spread fast and appealed by its discipline and asceticism to the samurai. In the history of Japanese printing the scattering of this culture through many temples caused the production of the first non-Buddhist works, the earliest medical book to be printed in Japan, and in 1590 a Japanese dictionary. In painted scrolls and thick-brush poems the Zen influence was revolutionary.

It is still delightful to take a train from Shinjuku station for Kamakura, and get out at Kita-Kamakura just a few miles beyond the seemingly uncontrolled edges of Tokyo. One arrives in country air, among trees; the train moves on to its next  stop, Kamakura. From this stretch of platform one takes a path along the track, past a few people selling maps, and up towards two of the historically splendid Zen temples of Kencho-ji and Engaku-ji. As ever among temples in Japan, peace comes dropping fast. Something or other will be blossoming, in defiance of the strict Zen discipline which seems to extend (as a national habit, not only at Zen temples) to tree-clipping. Water drips from high trees, in seasons I have witnessed; steep paths lead among the graves, bamboo rods protect other paths from visitors. In these tranquil places the doctrines of Zen were first brought to Japan.

The books printed at Zen temples are called *gozan-ban*. Among them the landmark dates from about 1364, the *Analects of Confucius*, honored as the first non-Buddhist work printed in Japan. One page from the edition *circa* 1400 reproduced in the Hyde catalogue impresses by its size, conviction and clarity. Non-Buddhist and non-sectarian works from the Zen temples take us to fresh woods and pastures new, the blossoming of different forms of art, printing, printed illustration and the new era of Ieyasu as first Tokugawa shogun.

Looking back to such evidence as is near me, writing at home, these early and unadorned Buddhist texts seem to have been little sought or discovered by collectors outside Japan. Nothing of the sort exists in the Spencer collection of the New York Public Library, or the Chester Beatty collection in Dublin: Philip Hofer, most perceptive of collectors and a hawk for opportunity, seeking treasure in Japan of the 1950s, had his focus only upon manuscript.

The Hyde collection, formed at the same time, was an interesting exception; not because Donald Hyde had any rare ability to recognize the qualities of early

CHAPTER ONE: EARLY PRINTING

Buddhist printing when he saw it, but for the admirable reason that he trusted the best of scholar-booksellers, Shigeo Sorimachi, who died at the age of 85 in 1991.

Bookshops in the Kanda district of Tokyo are still a pleasure, but a decreasing one. With knowledge of the Japanese language such visits might still be a delight, though extravagant. An hour or two at Mr. Sorimachi's house was a different and older experience, always with a younger friend who interpreted. Peace made itself felt; as one squatted at his low table, his wife shuffled in with tea and a sweet, and a stick to poke it with; and a mauve azalea lit the small garden outside. He sat perfectly upright, happy and precise. Would I perhaps like to see. . . unfortunately his finest things were locked in a warehouse, he is very sorry. . . minor hesitation, and one box among several is chosen. Peace thickens, with a niggle as to price.

When Mr. Hyde came to visit, Sorimachi explains, he accepted advice and bought for his collection whatever was proposed. A faint question-mark, as if I might conduct myself thus; but those were the days, and anyway Hyde was rich.

The relevant conclusion of this anecdote happened in New York on October 7, 1988. I was tempted to go there that eve of my birthday but it would have been a wasted journey. Christie's were selling the Hyde collection, generously given by Mary Hyde (Lady Eccles) to benefit the Morgan Library's appeal for its new building. I cannot conceal a strong sense that the library should have taken the collection, and left the building to bide its time—but such is ever the way with libraries. Always appeals and funds for another building, severely short in provision when it comes to books.

Mr. Sorimachi attended that occasion at Christie's and bought back most of what he had sold to Donald Hyde. It was a sensational "success," for the collecting world had changed. For once, I shall mention values (the tedious aspect of any book, essay, talk about collecting). That which came readily to Hyde in the 1950s and 60s, when nobody in the West wanted it and (therefore?) few Japanese showed interest, had become rare and suddenly very expensive. No doubt values will double and treble again, but for early Buddhist printing that was an October Revolution. The precious *Kasuga-ban* Lotus Sutra from mid-thirteenth century, estimate $20,000–30,000, sold for $143,000; a single volume (a scroll nearly 1,000 centimeters long), also from Kofuku-ji, *Kasuga-ban*, estimate $4,000–6,000, brought $33,000. A "Pure Land" volume (*Jodokyo-ban*) from the same period, estimate $3,000–4,000, produced $41,800. A religious work explaining Tendai Buddhism, printed in the last quarter of the thirteenth century at Hiei (*Hieizan-ban*), estimate $6,000–8,000, was also bought by Mr. Sorimachi for $41,800.

And so it continued, nothing more surprising than this new recognition, which the auctioneers had not perceived, of a wonderful and difficult focus for collectors.

As I write, that was five years ago. No such sale has occurred since, no such opportunity appeared. It stands as a monument to Mr. Sorimachi, whose name will recur in these chapters. He had advised Donald Hyde, who in his turn was wise enough to listen. The expensive and perceptive "dealer" (loathsome word) provides an incomparable haven for those who seek possession and education at once. It so happened, as witness Hofer's *Book Collector* article from Winter 1958, that in those years in Japan nothing was very expensive.

What of the future, in this obscure and absorbing subject? Between the time when the Hyde collection was formed under Mr. Sorimachi's advice, and 1988 when Sorimachi bid to all heights to get it back again, such books and scrolls had become rare. They still exist in temples; it is said that clandestine sales take place. In Koyasan I was able to buy scroll-paintings which the dealer boasted had come from local temples; he seemed to manage such arrangements without worry, the bureaucrats had not ascended. I would expect more detection of styles and the nuances of paper and ink, as between the productions of one and another temple, as scholars scrutinize with technical equipment in libraries which own such works. The gates of the field will then be wide open, but not to collectors because they would find no crop. Sheer dearth will spoil that ground, or the plague which goes with it, "national treasure."

Until very recently—October 1988 I suppose—it was possible to buy modestly in Japan printed sutra scrolls from the Kamakura period, of no identifiable origin but in remarkably good condition. Foolishly I parted with two: *never* let anything leave a collection, is the safest rule. Further back, from Harry Levinson, a perceptive and enterprising bookseller in Beverley Hills, I had a series of worm-eaten volumes (unrestored, one should say, original condition) said to have been set in movable type. That was before the notion of collecting had afflicted me. Exhibited in Tokyo, they were seized upon sight by Mr. Sorimachi. The same fate struck three most beautiful printed scrolls in an old box, which I had bought as dating from the tenth century. When a friend said they could not be earlier than the twelfth they went to a Tokyo book fair. Calm, upright Mr. Sorimachi could not hide his delight in discovering the objects and their price. There are two tales of folly which I regret and am unlikely to redeem.

1. Chibbett, p. 39
2. Chibbett, p. 106
3. Chibbett, p. 97
4. *Japanese Buddhist Prints*. English adaptation by Charles S. Terry. Tokyo and Palo Alto, 1963
5. "The use of *imbutsu* and *into* [printed Buddhas and pagodas], even when applied in the margins of texts, was intended for devotional, never artistic, purposes." Chibbett, p. 96

CHAPTER TWO
MANUSCRIPT EXAMPLES

Any exhibition at a Japanese temple, chosen from its early treasures, will show examples of manuscript sutras, beautifully written, which to a Western visitor seem impressively early: fragments in gold on blue paper perhaps, and whole scrolls in black on colorless paper from the eighth, ninth, tenth centuries, late-Nara or early-Heian periods. The frequent survival of these scrolls may be due to the immense number produced when Nara and Kyoto were over-staffed with priests who wrote them; but also, to the length of a single work. For example, a famous set of sutras at the Jingo-ji outside Kyoto, known as the *Tripitaka*, "must have included," we read in the Jackson Burke catalogue, "about five thousand scrolls." The writing of it "was started by the retired emperor Toba just before his death in 1156 and was completed in 1185 by his son, Goshirakawa, who lived at this temple after his abdication from the throne in 1158." The entire work was written in gold on the finest deep-blue paper, of the kind reserved (it is said) for imperial use.

One of those many scrolls from Jingo-ji is in front of me now, the red seal of Jingo-ji preceding the text. Each scroll has a frontispiece, as this has, of "the Buddha, flanked only by two monks and two Bodhisattvas, giving the sermon at Vulture Peak," drawn and painted in silver and gold on the blue. At the back of this is the title, and a large design of lotus flowers and leaves in gold and silver, with gold decorative borders. It survives from the twelfth century in near-perfect state, elegant

本事經卷第四

本事經二法品第二之二

三藏法師玄奘奉　制譯

吾從世尊聞　如是語苾芻當知　若有苾芻

省睡眠具念正知心常安住恬豫清淨於諸

善法善觀時宜而正修習如是苾芻減省睡

眠具念正知心常安住恬豫清淨於諸善法

善觀時宜而正修習於二果中隨證一果謂

於現法武證有餘依涅槃界或不還果爾時

世尊重攝此義而說頌曰

Plate 7. Opening of the gold-on-blue Jingo-ji sutra

calligraphy with ruled silver borders on the dark blue paper of even tone and enduring strength [Plate 7].

It was not an incomprehensibly bad idea to retire from the Court and live at Jingo-ji. To go there now, you take a long bus ride from Kyoto and climb an easy path; through the woods, past waterfalls, restaurants, picnic platforms, the usual tempting distractions of shops and stalls which sell rice-cake, soup, salt-dried fish; up to the plateau of temple buildings, above a wide view of untouched forest. One hopes it is also untenanted, for there is a custom at Jingo-ji of flinging little earthenware saucers from that plateau down to the forest, and with them one's cares. On

the day of my visit, all cares flung away, unfortunately the temple treasury was shut.

Here also is a long scroll on yellow paper, from a few years later, with strong black calligraphy of exceptional clarity. Block-printing, even in the *Kasuga-ban*, never managed to achieve such effects as this, nor is paper of such caliber made in Japan now. These early sutras on special papers, in fine calligraphy, present grave problems now for collectors.

It was therefore a surprise to find much earlier scrolls, beautifully written on white paper, which had not—and have not yet—attracted comparable attention from collectors in the West. That is always likely to apply equally in Japan, where taste follows foreign habits of fashion or discovery. It remains true that manuscript scrolls from the eighth and ninth centuries, unthinkable and unavailable in Europe, have not yet caught the imagination of Japanese collectors; they do not compare in value to those gold-on-blue manuscripts from three centuries later. Yet they occupy the first glass cases in such exhibits as the November Shoso-in at Nara, or treasures from the Horyu-ji, shown—on Thursdays when the weather is fine—in Tokyo.

Such scrolls have three marvellous qualities: antiquity, calligraphy and paper [Plate 8]. The paper, not glamorous, brownish-white, remains perfectly strong and crackles healthily as one opens it. The text, as the Chester Beatty example (No. 204, illustrated in that catalogue), is from the *Daihannya-Kyo* or—if one chooses to pronounce the transliteration from Sanskrit—the *Mahaprajnaparamita Sutra*. In the Kamakura period a complete set of the sutra was owned by a priest who signed his name after the colophon of many of the scrolls, with the comment that he had marked it in red. His red blobs, marking passages which struck him as noteworthy, remain clear for us to see. As Christopher De Hamel remarked to me, "where in

Europe would one find an eighth-century manuscript, with known provenance from the twelfth century?"

On the last occasion when I chose two of these scrolls, sitting opposite Mr. Sakai at Isseido, his father was present and asked a stern question. "My father wishes to know why you want these sutras, because you are not a Buddhist." News of my interest had spread within hours, as appeared in conversation that evening at a meeting of the Grolier Club of Japan.

Paper, calligraphy, piety endured, as acts of grace. Some years ago I had the not particularly bright idea, as a bookseller, of seeking other examples of *Hyakumanto Darani*, those little pagodas with their printed "charms" from the eighth century, and bought several in Tokyo. At Culham the great Dr. Kawase in a memorable visit declared one to be forged—quite undetectable to my eye, but of course I accepted his verdict and sadly returned it; the menace of forgery exists. In Jimbo-cho the bookseller, no doubt very irritated, behaved with perfect courtesy; and I, having spent money and being in Tokyo, entered his shop as if possessing a fine large book-token, ready to exchange the errant object for something delicious.

So here is one of those enchanting and extra-curricular works of art, a gold-on-blue scroll from the early seventeenth century (that period of aesthetic renaissance) in its lacquer box with the imperial chrysanthemum emblem (adopted and adapted

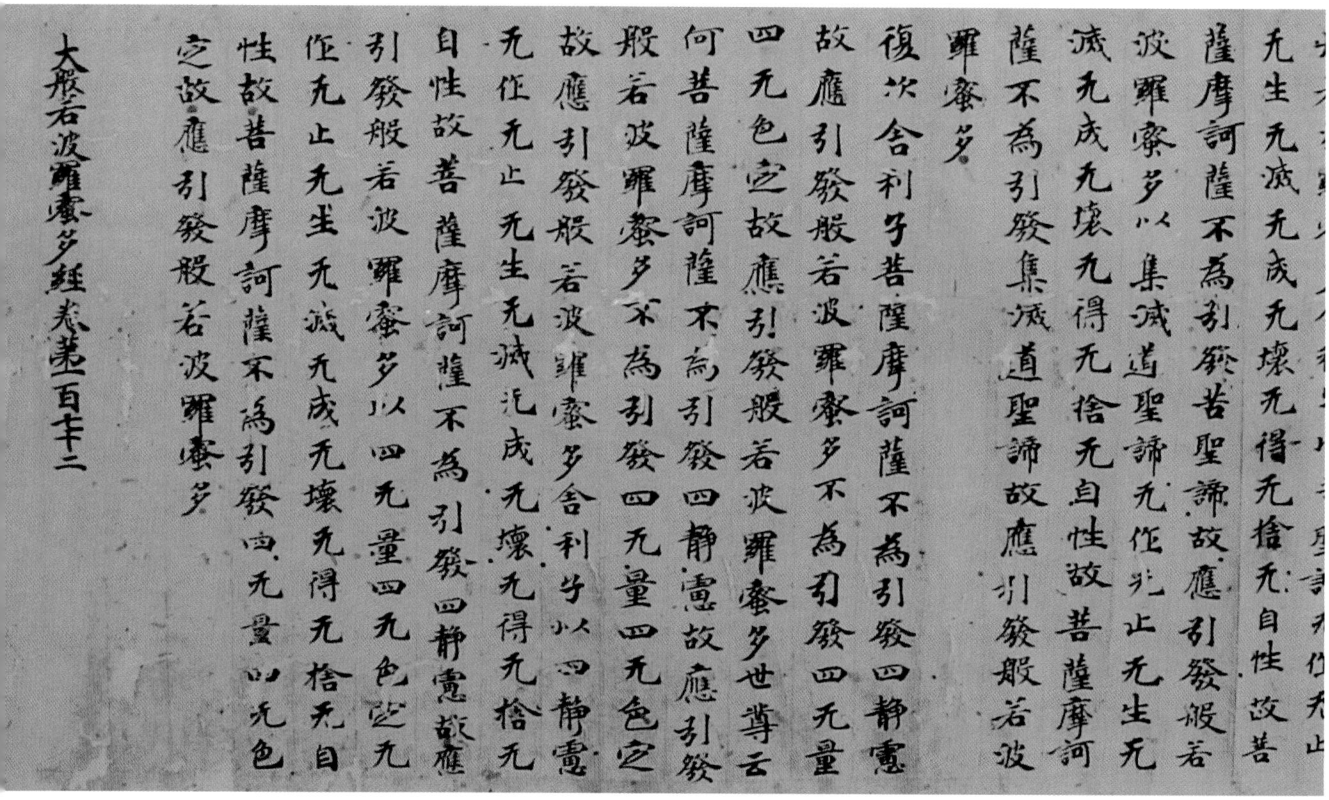

Plate 8. Colophon of a Nara-period scroll

CHAPTER TWO: MANUSCRIPT EXAMPLES

by Rossetti and Beardsley) in mother-of-pearl and gold asymmetrically; a gift from the shogun Ieyasu's granddaughter to one of the temples at Nikko [Plate 9]. The sutra is written within ruled borders of silver and gold; the intricate frontispiece, of Buddha with many of his disciples—I count twenty-four, in various phases of enlightened activity—is in fine-line of gold on gold, with minimal use of bronze and blue, and hair-thin black outline for the shapes of heads. The back of the scroll is gold, with occasional blue circles of lotus leaves. I can only feel surprised by the priests at Nikko who surrendered it, and grateful to Dr. Kawase for detecting a forged *Hyakumanto Darani*.

The pleasure of a Japanese manuscript will not come from comprehension, and need not concern illustration. Two more examples of this nature, for different reasons, are relevant. I had viewed with helpless desire the multi-colored papers of poetry scrolls at the Tokyo National Museum, and more recently the wonderful Ise Monogatari, beyond my reach at the Isseido bookshop. Some years ago Mr. Sorimachi showed me a very fair consolation prize, the seventeenth-century manuscript of a Noh play written out by the leading actor of that moment, on superb paper—colored a daring orange, alternating with grey-white, painted throughout in gold and silver with flowers and grasses, birds, Fuji, the moon [Plate 10]. Its covers are deep blue, with night-paintings of gold; paintings of mountain, mist, tree and waterfall in gold and black adorn the inside covers, within gold-sprayed borders. The play's author was a fourteenth-century ancestor of the actor-scribe.

加様に作れ共ハみ濃田野上の物の
長して従梅を成立花子や上鵬候得
通いて過て作い過して春乃比較より
左画乃廿將風してやらにや
いらゝに此宿に侍と雨うまる彼
花子を隈う清妻乃乃作るゝ扇
波ーゝつて切り作にしゝゝわ花子扇に

This beautiful manuscript ends before five leaves which cannot be called blank; rather it fades into the colored and painted pages with no text, the whole performance expressing, with more eloquence even than *Saga-bon* plays but from that same moment, the courtly provenance of *Noh*.

My other, non-pictorial example is very different. Three centuries of Tokugawa rule date from the very end of the sixteenth century, the Battle of Sekigahara, when the first Tokugawa shogun, Ieyasu, triumphed. We climb among opulent shrines at Nikko and visit his memorial, to this day. Here is a manuscript of small aesthetic merit, a short letter in large *hiragana* script in scroll form, mounted on gold-and-silver-clouded paper—from Ieyasu to several of his generals, written on the eve of the battle of Sekigahara. He tells them to hold their ground for he is coming to their assistance. The four generals to whom copies are sent are named at the end—as in a modern letter, "Copies to . . . ." The message itself concludes with the powerful *mon* in his own hand, of Ieyasu. This document, one is aware, introduced the great Edo period, and now may suitably raise a curtain upon its books.

Plate 10 (preceding pages). Inside cover and opening of a Noh manuscript, early Edo period

CHAPTER THREE
PAINTED BOOKS I

WHEN we escape from basic European fascination with movable type and woodblock color-printing, the greater pleasure lies in Japanese painted books: album, scroll and codex.

Emaki, scrolls with text and illustrations, have the longest history. The advances and advantages of books as codices, with pages to flip forward and backward for facts and to find one's place, are obvious; so is a defiance of those practical points, evident in the thousand-year history of painted and hand-written scrolls in Japan. Painted scrolls reduce our tempo; they are for slow viewing, a deliberate nuisance—as is their preparation, compared with multiple prints from wood.

The other phrase in my vocabulary is *Nara-ehon*, meaning Nara picture books: a term still difficult to define, said to have been coined early in the twentieth century by—perish the thought—"rare books dealers." Much of an essay by a Japanese art-historian, Yutaka Shimizu, translated into English and published by Dawson's of Los Angeles in 1960,[1] is given to arguing for and against this or that meaning of the phrase. Whole scrolls, it is suggested, being long and expensive—a single work commonly extending to three scrolls and more—*Nara-ehon* provided abbreviated versions, in book form, for more popular use.

It will be appreciated by those who wander about Japan, even now, that space and resource for books existed in very few homes of that feudal society; yet if the scroll with its length of paintings may be imagined as chopped into pages, reduced and abbreviated, the possibility of oblong books arrives. Such were the early Nara picture books: not very sophisticated in style, multi-volume, small. I recall a morning in Mr. Sorimachi's house, when just such a set was produced and—a rare event—he commended it to me. These small blue-paper-covered oblongs, with their fairly crude illustrations, silver and gold smudged and smeared upon them, held little appeal as I viewed them then—regrettably, as is now clear. A general rule of life should have been to accept gratefully the suggestions of Mr. Sorimachi in the privilege of a visit to his home. They were *Nara-ehon* of the earlier kind, late sixteenth or very early seventeenth century, before the high finish and luxury of Edo period work. An example of that simple sort, near to folk art, now seems deeply desirable.

"An *emaki* must illustrate a text," says Miyeko Murase in her introduction to the catalogue of a great exhibition of them in Japan, published by the Asia Society in 1983. In that exhibition, examples from the twelfth to the twentieth century were divided into six categories: "sacred texts, romantic tales (*monogatari*), popular tales (*setsuwa*), portraits, biographies of celebrated priests, and histories of temples and shrines (*engi*)." All were picture scrolls with texts, styles of painting and proportion of painting to calligraphy varying greatly.

We may look first at the subject which is simpler, because its chronology (though not its meaning) rests within easier limits: *Nara-ehon*. Why Nara? It seems the monks who illustrated religious scrolls, being less than fully occupied, had long been allowed to paint for members of the court. They painted fans; Nara fans evolved in a style of their own, from the under-employed artist priests, similar to that which I saw at Mr. Sorimachi's house and so foolishly rejected.

Whatever their origin, such books were made in fairly large numbers during the sixteenth century and a little later—as were illuminated Books of Hours in France, after most other forms of Western book had been claimed by the printing press. The motive, a lingering delight in color and luxury, was comparable.

At the start of the Edo period, some political stability encouraged or happened to coincide with a phase of elegance, as expressed in the *Saga-bon* books and a new kind of *Nara-ehon* which had much in common with the most precise, finished style of Persian and Indian miniatures. It struck me in first seeing these, that whereas one may be fortunate to own two or three such miniatures, in Japan it was still possible to find marvellous examples of complete volumes or whole works illuminated thus, instead of individual leaves extracted from them.

As with the Persians and Indians, the books are generally anonymous. Unlike the prints and printed albums, artists' names remained unknown; I was told that may have been why *Nara-ehon* were not more keenly collected in the West—even in Japan—though such comment now sounds sadly out of date. Wealth spread from feudal *daimyo* limits, and beauty was needed to represent it. In such a climate *Nara-ehon* became part of the bride's dowry—as had Books of Hours, a little earlier, in France.

This pleasant state of affairs existed for about a century, from perhaps 1620 to 1720. There seems no better reason than fashion for its decline and disappearance, in a land where painstaking arts conspicuously flourished. Such was the history of *Nara-ehon*, an art reaching its height in the late seventeenth century and recognized only in recent years.

"They represent," says the catalogue of the Ryerson collection, "the transitory stage between old scroll works and the books with printed illustrations which were published after the seventeenth century." That perhaps provides as good a theory as any for the disappearance of *Nara-ehon* after the middle Edo period. The argument from democracy, to explain their earlier existence, is also convincing; but in that first century of Tokugawa rule, our seventeenth century, these beautifully illuminated manuscripts shifted from folk art to high elegance.

The best were of two kinds, recognizable at once by their size and binding: the larger and earlier, with gold-painted covers of that dark blue paper used for the finest early sutras, and gold paste-downs, came in three volumes measuring about twelve inches by nine and a half [Plate 11]. For such patrician manuscripts, the paper—in the example I am looking at, anyway, and in another I have most regrettably parted with—was a thin *torinoko*, described by Yutaka Shimizu as being "a smooth, faintly yellow paper resembling the shell of a chicken's egg," made

Plate 11. *Cover, Bun-sho Monogatari (Nara-chou)*

from *gampi* (*Wikstroemia gampi*) and mulberry bark. Close-textured and strong, it still crackles when moved or turned. Discreetly gold-painted with forms of landscape, fruit and grasses, fine calligraphy was mandatory and, one hopes, a pleasure.

The illustrations are full-page, or double-page, with no blank margin. These paintings, always in the Japanese or Tosa style, view domestic scenes as if there were no roofs and the artist could watch from a short distance above. Top and bottom are stylized bands of cloud, scattered gold over pale blue. Though they tell the episodes of a story, such pages are carefully composed groups, deputations,

performances, occasionally journeys and landscape; where the moments recorded are indoors, screens provide landscape. So one's pleasure comes from the wonderful variety of color in gowns and kimonos, patterned with gold; in solid lacquered black for the trailing hair of women which, when they sit in groups, makes its own rhythm; or—with the focus upon detail—in the very fine brushwork of pattern upon pattern, even black upon black, in the clothes. Brilliance of color was essential: red, orange, gold for young women; blacks, blues, greys for the men, solid green ground indoors and out [Plate 12].

Printed books, as the Ryerson catalogue suggests, had nothing of this sort to offer at such a date; they were venturing into orange and green hand-tinting here and there, a form of woodcut illustration called *tanroku* much prized (i.e., highly expensive) now among collectors but a million miles from illumination in *Nara-ehon*. And though detail and color characterize them, an instinct for apt composition leaves no doubt that the best were done by incomparable artists. An uneasy sense that one ought to be looking at black Zen blots cannot conceal the truth that I view these books with more delight than all others, East or West.

Another kind is here, of equal refinement and only slightly later, in silk-brocade bindings and many volumes [Plates 13–15]. The page is smaller (11.5" x 8.5"), the story longer and its episodes more varied: similar *torinoko* paper, arrangements of people and trailing hair, patterning of black on black of silks, red on red, and the Tosa roofless style of painting. This must be from mid-seventeenth century, with more variety of color, ever bright, and repose in composition though it tells an active story. The legend is of Shotoku-Taishi, whose real name was Prince Umayado, born miraculously to the mouth of Ohoye as her second son according to the word and promise of the Buddhist god Kannon. Living from 574 to 622 A.D., he received the title Shotoku or "Holy Goodness" after his death, in honor of his brave opposition to local Shinto revolts against Buddhism, which had recently arrived from Korea and China.

So these volumes relate his life of courage in opposing the rebels and their iconoclasm as Buddhist images were destroyed, burned, hurled into the sea; the marvellous arrival of human help floating down on clouds from the sky, and upon other clouds a fiery dragon. Again there are no margins, only a formal suggestion of mist across the top and bottom of each picture, flecked with gold. And the key to such paintings, action packed or ceremonial, tranquil or cruel, is (apart from color and technique) the calm and detachment of perfect placement. Faces show no anger, agony or surprise; rescue rides down from the clouds as if exercising in Hyde Park; battles are splendid from the grouping of horses and a miniaturist's execution of his art in brilliant detail upon armor. From energetic war we move

Plate 12. From the Bun-sho Monogatari *(early blue covers)*

35

Plate 13. From the Shotoku-Taishi Nara-ehon, Volume I

without changing key to the preparation of a feast, students of calligraphy, all the opulence of reception at court, and the paraphernalia of royal journeys and priestly processions.

This was indeed an extraordinary moment in the history of books; well aware that gold is not art, I know none of greater elegance than this in color, composition, material, and the skills of miniature painting. Calligraphy, in the running hand or *hiragana*, in such a work is dependably excellent. To enjoy it one has no need to read, which would be beyond the scope of most Japanese viewers, as was mentioned earlier.

The reason for taking what then seemed a large decision in Tokyo was that Mr. Sakai of the booksellers Isseido urged us to do so. As with Mr. Sorimachi, it would generally (nobody can say *always*) have been sensible to accept advice from precious experience. Many years ago in the strongroom at H.P. Kraus in New York, when I hesitated and dithered over a large folio of manifest beauty and excellence from the early sixteenth century, Hans Kraus said with characteristic emphasis "I *order* you to buy that book," and I obeyed. Best books in the best shops are not likely to be serious blunders. The flowering of *Nara-ehon* in mid-seventeenth century, which must seem to most of us its peak, was caused by the availability of artists, sudden freedom of a stable society, and fashion among a large number of affluent families; it produced, until color-printing became competitive, a century of secular illuminated manuscripts, inadequately known as yet in the West—comparable with the finest Persian or Indian examples.

Another similar work which is here, longer than the last and from the same moment, prompts a comment about that puzzling subject, completeness. This manuscript recalls Kyoto, with a member of my family who speaks Japanese asking in one or another likely shop whether they could show any *Nara-ehon*: no, no, no. We ended at a part-art-gallery-part-bookshop, with the same uncomprehending negative until its powerful director said he could show something if we didn't mind waiting. We waited. Enter, after forty minutes, staff from the first shop we had visited, carrying the object which is beside me now, and several scrolls I have forgotten.

The smart black lacquer box, its title on top in thick gold, holds ten brocade-bound volumes of what I was seeking, in abundance: the same size as those blue brocade volumes, but fatter and fuller; counting now they have one hundred and eleven pages of paintings, and seven double-pages [Plate 16]. Calligraphy, again on *torinoko* paper with grass-and-flower backgrounds of gold, is of greater precision and refinement than in the other. As this seemed too good to be true, I remember travelling impatiently leaf by leaf through the whole work expecting a disappointment of worm or smudge; but there was none. Unable really to afford such treasure I bought it for a collector who could well afford it. He has never been allowed to see it.

Some while later a group of Japanese visitors informed me with pleasure that the complete work would have run to fourteen volumes. Without reducing the delight

Plate 14. From the Shotoku-Taishi Nara-ehon, Volume III

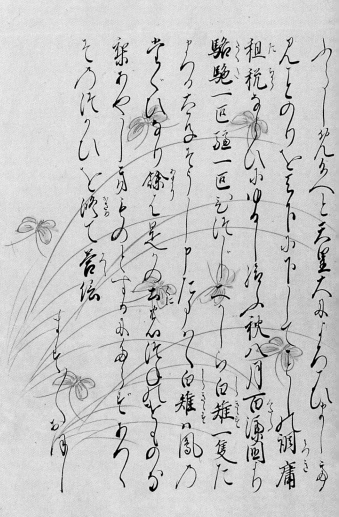

of what was here, this infuriated me; for I should have been told, and wrote to the gallery-owner in Kyoto, who sent an equivocal reply. Within a year I was there again with my son Gideon, and the three of us enjoyed a long argument on the grand scale. The dealer put his view that Japanese people see this rather for art than completeness, I mine that if he offers an incomplete work I should be told. There was no thought of returning these wonderful volumes to him. Whether from conscience or courtesy, he returned some of the price.

I do not know which of us was right; the English traveller always supposes he is deceived. When we first looked at painted scrolls (some of which may also be called *Nara-ehon*) in Tokyo a delightful and much-respected bookseller, who seemed surprised by our interest, received us in his home dressed in traditional clothes. Politely he showed a tempting and beautiful work in three scrolls; but as he showed it, I noticed one text seemed abbreviated, perhaps one of the paintings also. Examining the scrolls as if this had not struck him before, he agreed with me—and explained, through my wife who understands the language well enough, that it is not a point which worries Japanese people. Stupidly, I left those scrolls with him.

These essays concern collecting, so I present the matter with some uncertainty; there is no absolute advice. The time will come when people will collect Japanese miniatures as they now collect Persian and Indian—as increasingly they collect leaves and painted initials from Western illuminated

Plate 15. From the Shotoku-Taishi Nara-ehon, *Volume IV*

manuscripts. Temples in Japan are forbidden to sell their paintings and scrolls now, which is not to say that it never happens. Japanese shopkeepers chop *emaki* to pieces, mounting the fragments within brocade borders upon scrolls to hang above the small shrines which grace many Japanese homes.

On the other hand, from Mr. Sorimachi I chose a box with two long and astonishing scrolls painted on silk, which will be mentioned below; the complete work had a third scroll. When I questioned this, he made it clear that, if complete, it

Plate 16. Scene of peace from the Kyoto Nara-ehon

would not have been there for me to see—and I could not have afforded to buy it. The debate is open to the house. I am puzzled by the neurosis of European collectors as to completeness, values dropping with a thump if a book they cannot comprehend lacks one leaf of text. Japan, in this, is as yet undecided. Meanwhile, and considering *Nara-ehon*, nobody objects to completeness; in a long work with so many paintings of such merit, perfectly surviving, it is not a subject to keep one awake at night.

These volumes are action-packed; but whether heads being struck off or priests in contemplation, horses dashing, women weeping, music playing or kings feasting, the artist's greater concern—calm, temple-trained—was in placing people, screens, hills, the color-on-color and patterning of clothes. Battle and armor become decorative design. No saint met death with such indifference as both sides in these troubles display. Kimonos lifted to the eyes express extreme grief. A hint of character in male faces distinguishes this book's style from the last; the school of art, and many scenes chosen for illustration, are identical through two quite different stories—deputations received, priests at their calligraphy, feasting while servants concealed behind an awning prepare the fish; and always these astounding colors, basic green, the brilliance of clothes arranged in contrast. It was as if, at the time of *Saga-bon* and *tanroku* books, this was done to beat them to a cocked hat. As they were formal treasures carefully kept, we should expect survival in perfect state. I do not hesitate to place a display of such refinement above Utamaro's willowy girls in multiple blocks, color-printed.

1. *Nara Picture Books*, translated by Richard Zumwinkle

CHAPTER FOUR

PAINTED BOOKS II

Iт would not now be possible to collect illuminated manuscript narrative scrolls—*emaki*—from the sixteenth century or earlier, the pre-Tokugawa period. In the 1983 exhibition catalogue mentioned above, we read:

> There are many reasons why an exhibition that focuses exclusively on *emaki* has never been attempted outside of Japan before. Primary among these are the difficulties inherent in assembling a group of Japan's most prized cultural treasures.

So, we must see them for the most part in museums, where *emaki* may be displayed more satisfactorily than books, which can only reveal a single opening. Museum cases allow the unrolling of these works to vast footage, though half a dozen in a room devoted to several forms of art take up much of the available space. Notably splendid, often changed, examples may be seen as part of the Freer collection in Washington and at the Tokyo National Museum, Ueno Park. The new museum, MOA Bijutsukan in Atami, an hour south of Tokyo by train, has memorably elegant black-ink scrolls, *sumiyoshi*, from the sixteenth century in its permanent collection. Fragments from a famous eleventh-century *emaki* of the *Genji Monogatari*, commercially taken apart and sold long ago, were assembled again and exhibited recently at the Suntory Museum in Tokyo. If early *emaki* appear for sale now they are likely to be declared "national treasure," not for export.

One example is here, having surfaced not long ago in California—early, incomplete and greatly intriguing: scenes from that epic thirteenth-century battle between

Plate 17. From the large album of paintings and calligraphy (section)

the two powerful clans, Taira and Minamoto, which heralded the start of the Kamakura period [Plate 18]. A point of fascination is the total contrast of style compared with those detailed and decorative battle paintings, all focusing upon design and the pattern of armor, in the late-seventeenth century *Nara-ehon*. Here the emphasis is force, torture (daggers slicing out eyes) and the swiftness of action on horseback, leading to powerful compositions where foreground hills sometimes

Plate 18. Battle scene in the mysterious "California" scroll

hide all but heads, shoulders and swords. Wounded warriors tumble upside-down from their horses, and faces are large, almost grotesque, as against the later sophistication which grouped them in masses detached from particular incident.

Yet this old scroll shows the clan leader and his generals eating, as behind a foreground awning two servants prepare—chop up—fish and a bird; while to the left, not far away, one of those unpleasant eye operations is performed. It impresses as desperate action; two horsemen, bows drawn, shoot as they gallop at frantic speed through the high grasses. As art, it is a lesson in the use of scrolls which should indeed be viewed between both hands at a table; thus each passage holds interest, the composition varies, action unfolds as at the cinema. Thirty-six feet under glass in a museum can never produce that effect, or such surprises.

Scrolls are not quite easy to handle, only more or less difficult. Closing one end as the other is opened, many follow a tiresome habit of rolling up crooked; then they must be opened and scrolled again, not knocked straight. When the spindle or axis is long enough to be held, this becomes easier; often they are not, for reasons understood by their makers, but patience rather than speed in this subject is well rewarded. Scrolls need and induce calm of mind.

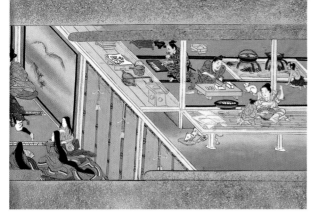

Plate 19. In the kitchen, Iwaya Monogatari

If early sixteenth-century *Nara-ehon* were a kind of popular shortening of scrolls into books, it must be agreed that in the late seventeenth century there was not much to choose between them; one family preferred its bridal present in traditional scroll form, another commissioned a similar work of art as stitched volumes, bound usually with brocade or gold-painted indigo paper. The more luxurious productions, anyway, were similar. From Mr. Sorimachi my earliest choice was the work in front of me, three scrolls in the most refined calligraphy, the illustrations as one unrolls them on a rather larger scale than was convenient upon separated pages of books but comparable in style, concentrating on color, pattern and arrangement rather than human emotions of the story.

It was natural for a scroll to spread wide, taking the eye across a composition, though any part of it could also be viewed in detail; the miniaturist exercised his skills within one page or over a single opening. Brocade outside, gold paper within, and gold-patterned orange paper for the calligraphic title slips were identical. There are three grades of *torinoko* paper, Yutaka Shimizu tells us: thin, medium and thick. The thick grade was used for these three scrolls, strong to hold, with gold-painted tree forms and grasses behind all the text or gold

Plate 20. Section of the Nara-ehon scroll, Iwaya Monogatari

scattered like snow storms. The survival of such works in marvellous condition is evidence of occasional use and reverent handling. It is the *Iwaya Monogatari* [Plates 19–20], a story summarized thus by Watson in his article on such narratives:

> The daughter of a Chunagon was oppressed by a stepmother. Eventually the girl is cast away on an island in the Awaji sea, where she is rescued by a seaman called Akashi, who feeds and lodges her in a cave. Later a Lieutenant-General, second son of the Kampaku, finds the girl and takes her to the capital where she is honoured as a Kampaku's wife.

But it is all there to be seen: the girl exiled, rowed away from shore; the prince happening upon her, peeping over a brushwood fence to watch; her return and welcome home as his betrothed; an archetypal legend recalling Perdita and Florizel of *The Winter's Tale.*

Plate 21 (following pages). Saintly trial before triumph, from the Kitano-Tsuya Monogatari

A little later, large and heavy, painted on silk and mounted, the two volumes provided by Mr. Sorimachi in a modern box made to fit them tell the *Kitano-Tsuya Monogatari* [Plates 21–23]. They show an entirely different style of painting, Chinese and formal, "with wide sweeps," I wrote after seeing it for the first time, "of semi-melancholy coloring." Width and height impress, each subject becoming almost a major work. The story is of religious pilgrimage. In the first scroll we follow a priest, in one

Plate 22. Peace and scholarship, Kitano-Tsuya Monogatari

of those composite paintings such as were common in medieval Europe, walking undamaged through the fires of hell to a state of grace and peace beyond. As between Buddhist and Christian hell, with fierce judges enjoying themselves among their appalling accusations and tortures, there was little to differentiate.

Wide spaces, silks and beautiful coloring of this *emaki* provide a different kind of experience; as does the large *hiragana* calligraphy over leaves, fruit and tendrils which develop from gold-painted background to colored persimmon and orchids.

Plate 23. Calligraphy over fruit decoration on silk, Kitano-Tsuya Monogatari

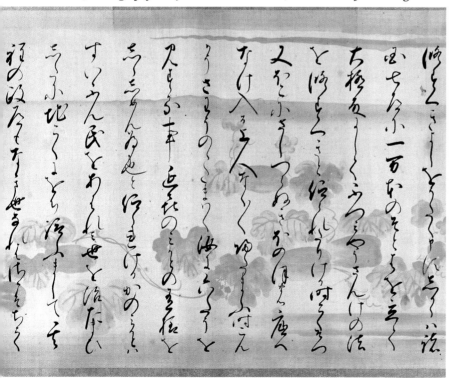

The opening and closing of such heavy objects demand a slow pace; appreciation arrives with dignity—no indecorous riffling through for the high-spots. These paintings seem too long for Japanese furniture, for they were unlikely to have been viewed as I see one now, in a single sweep. This style could never have been reduced into oblong pages of any book. It represents a formal event, such as we shall not properly understand; our tables and museum cases alike distort.

The handling and viewing of Japanese scrolls, books and prints is a subject worth discussing, from these heavy scrolls to a framed triptych. Opening a scroll always seems relatively quick and simple; rolling it up again needs practice, for its nature is to travel crooked and loose. That problem solved, the single tape of woven silk is wound to the limit and tucked under itself, and a good scroll should be wrapped in silk within its wooden box. Practice makes less imperfect; in Japan one watches with envy as library staff in white coats perform the operation clinically.

Japanese books have stitched paper covers, and chapters are written about traditional stitching methods; but as I can never understand them, there would be no point in trying to explain. Our phrase "original boards" is not appropriate, for they used no boards but protected a book with *chitsu*, loose cloth-board folders fastened by two small pieces of whale-bone slipped through cloth loops. Much care was given to the stitched covers, to their embossed patterns or woodblock designs, or simply to the character and color of paper. Such may survive the years in reasonable condition, with their old title slips—a pleasant surprise if one recalls illustrations by Bumpo, Kiho and others, of readers at peace in the open air with their books rolled double in one hand for easy reading.

More interesting (pausing at this lay-by on the road through painted books and albums) is the problem of margins across a double-page opening illustrating a single subject: two apparently separate prints, within their own borders, forming one picture. It was the custom, not always followed, to leave white space for the inner margins or gutter of a book. That practice has been extended to the different context of prints framed for hanging domestically or in a gallery: white space is observed between each separate print of a continuous picture. I am convinced this does not represent the true idea. Survival of many of the finer books in good condition suggests they were always meant to be handled carefully, not doubled back or pressed

Plate 24. A float in the ceremonial procession, Gion Shrine

flat. If you open a book carefully, without pressure, the bulge left and right hides those inner margins so that the whole picture is seen at a glance as artists and block-cutters intended. This is not received theory, but as one who handles books with excessive care I believe it to be so.

As to the scrolls known as *emaki*, painted and without text, they lent themselves easily to records of ceremonial procession and any serial activity viewed slowly as the action proceeds. Here is a work of extreme detail from the seventeenth century showing the annual progress towards the Gion Shrine in Kyoto: a form of carnival in spring, with traditional carts and floats which still exist, acrobats and animals, representatives of trades and clans in ancient dress [Plates 24–25]. Like a Lord Mayor's Show, on they go across three long scrolls of gold and many colors, fine-brush pattern equalling the skills of those who balanced upon the high tops of elaborate carriages and upon each other. The nearest modern comparison in my experience would be a night of carnival in Rio de Janeiro. Fantasy and luxury share the scene

Plate 25. Entrance to the ceremonial procession, Gion Shrine

with half-naked strong men pulling the loads; gold cloud, colored crowd in the familiar Nara style of that time. I have seen screens from that moment or a little later, painted all over with books in various states of fold and unfold, tied and unscrolled showing such scenes in illustration. The same artists, we may be sure, were equally engaged upon all or any.

Painted scrolls provided simple information, as for instance to show kinds of flower and insect. A scroll of whales, with no more than caption for text, has delighted my grandchildren as it opens slowly to reveal ever more surprising creatures, an educational work for Japan as bird recognition in Europe. Another subject often seen was mining for gold in the small island of Sado, one scroll showing the whole procedure and life of a mine, the washing and panning, melting, inspection and weighing. Scrolls in their formality offer a sense of occasion, different from one's approach to pages of a bound book.

* * * * *

NARA-EHON had its period, but the lives of Japanese painted books continued through the nineteenth century and after, delightful in themselves, the artists unthreatened by new techniques. Nothing so calms the spirit on a dim morning as looking through painted albums from Japan.

The album was a Chinese device. On visiting the vast museum of Chinese imperial treasures in Taiwan, album leaves provided my greatest pleasure: single openings, paintings facing poems, dismembered from larger groups. That was one way to view them, but albums could be made like books, or for turning fold by fold or stretched to their length as a screen; and such screens may extend like long scrolls. The need to see at a museum suggests again glass cases down a gallery half the length of a cricket pitch; but if that seems inappropriate for scrolls, it certainly reduces the pleasure and purpose of an album.

A major example rests on my left arm, from the first decade of the nineteenth century: late, aristocratic, traditional. Daimyo families commissioned such work—paintings and calligraphy on silk and many decorative papers—by a spectrum of artists and poets. Opened like a screen (mounted on gold, both sides, upwards of a hundred examples) the effect is lost. Two, contrasted, are enough for eyes and mind; there is no peace in the spectacle of so much variety seen as if it were a single work [Plate 26]. Thus the pleasant problem of how to handle Japanese books exists also among painted albums.

I do not know whether these paintings and poems were juxtaposed according to any scheme or style, but prefer to recall William Morris's conviction that objects good of their kind mix well together. As this rests now, a wild hunting scene below Fuji faces perfect tranquillity: the poet beside a pile of books looks wisely into the distance; at his back, facing away, a young boy blows the *sho*, that haunting mini-organ of bamboo pipes heard at

Plate 26. Opposing pages from the large album of painting and calligraphy

Shinto ceremonies; the poet leans against an ancient pine [Frontispiece]. A couple of turns further: to the left, the eternal idea of a pavilion above waters of a lake, sheltering trees under snow apparently, mountains and sky in moonlight expressed by a scattering of gold dust; opposite, a traditional Zen subject in thick ink lines with a little pink, the fat short-sighted priest stooping to read his scroll; while in front of him we see a graceful patient goat [Plates 17 & 26]. Wisteria on gold-flecked silk faces thick-brush black-ink calligraphy on paper; a brief poem on pink tinted paper, mottled as with heavy raindrops, faces a smug small duck of perfect brushwork and no outline, floating above a dead leaf larger than itself; infants spin-ning their top (painted by Bumpo) face a longer poem on silk; painting and painting, or simply the opposed styles of calligraphy, silk and varied papers. This is not matter for a May morning, but diversion for the tedium of winter evenings. Like Cleopatra, age shall not weary them nor custom stale their infinite variety. One poem on especially rare paper, gold-barred, red-textured, is mounted on brocade like a hanging scroll, against the gold ground. It is all a book-development from the screen idea, comedy and poetry mixing as in Shakespeare's theatre.

One other form of painted book, surviving and evolving for different reasons, reached its peak in the late Edo period and gives great pleasure because the skills existed: albums, folding or as books, of flowers, birds and insects. The need for true color caused them, for though printing offered artistic range it could not achieve scientific accuracy. In Europe, chromolithography for better and worse had been developed by mid-nineteenth century; luckily it arrived very late in Japan, where aquatint and stipple were never practiced.

So, we find books or albums of flowers and birds, painted with the excellence and elegance of Redouté [Plate 27]. Upon such paper as was available in Japan, or on silk, these works of art and science often follow a habit of asymmetry, spilling from the page as if edges were cropped. As the purpose was accuracy, and the painters anonymous, it is a vein of Japanese collecting which has not been much explored.

This chapter can end with one brief recollection of shopping in Kyoto, by way of advice to collectors. Japanese manners are closer to the French, I believe, than to English or American. At a Kyoto gallery we asked to see paintings, scrolls, explained that we were "seriously interested." After we viewed and dismissed negligible examples, the flower-and-bird *emaki* in front of me now was produced. In England,

Plate 27. Marrow fruit and flowers, from nine volumes of flower paintings

a spoken regret at parting from treasures may strike the ear as less than wholly sincere; in Paris and Kyoto the notion of only letting paintings or books, as if they were dogs, go to good homes, could still be part of a performance played with more spirit. I like the decorous assumption, in buying, of honor received rather than bestowed.

This scroll [Plate 28] represents art of a kind different from the scientific flower and bird works mentioned above; for groups and friends met to paint *kaben* (flower petals) and *choju* (birds and animals) in the early nineteenth century, as others gathered to write poems that became privately printed, beautifully designed *surimono*. Masuyama Sessai (1755–1820), daimyo of Nagashima in Ise, painted on silk the example here, a long composition of flowers, birds and leaves accurately observed and perfectly colored, to be opened slowly or seen as panorama. "His residence," according to Mitchell, "was frequented by many visitors—Bunjin and fashionable people;" salon life at a daimyo castle, in Kyoto of the late-Edo period—he died aged sixty-five in 1820. From such painting, and the Shijo books, it is possible to imagine a social spectrum before Japan became swamped by change.

Plate 28. Section of a scroll on silk by Masuyama Sessai, with his signature

CHAPTER FIVE

ILLUSTRATED BOOKS I

ANYONE looking through those two splendid quarto volumes by Jack Hillier published in 1987, *The Art of the Japanese Book*, will recognize the folly of attempting an essay on the subject here. It is a complex matter, with its many "schools" and influences, hundreds of artists and thousands of illustrated books.

A few points of reference become prominent. These are rather assemblies of wood-cut prints than illustrated books, approachable therefore for an ignorant foreigner. As with illuminated manuscripts or aquatints, coming through centuries in the darkness of shut books they have not faded—a great advantage over single prints and drawings which, commonly exposed, lose much of their color. Mauves and pinks, frequently used, were especially fugitive in the light.

Printing presses were not known in Japan. All of these illustrations, cut in wood blocks like the text, needed infinite skill of inking, less here and more there, and rubbing—the method was like brass-rubbing. Before that came the block-cutter, anonymous hero of this enterprise, who interpreted the drawing. Pure line was traced, but the gradations and brush-effects which created the qualities we most admire in so many of these books were unimaginably brilliant. Perhaps names do not much matter: we know and classify the designers, knowing almost nothing about these practitioners who created their work. In the fine and famous books nothing was automatic, but those who made them are usually left in shadow.

The many "schools" to which designers—better to call them artists—belonged, or from which they claimed descent, are so confusing that I shall lazily, on the whole, ignore them. Though it may not be too difficult to learn definitions of Tosa, Kano, Nanga, Rimpa, Maruyama, Shijo, the nuisance comes from an excess of cross-fertilization. It is not a simple matter like bird-recognition. One or another artist perhaps started in the Kano school, switched to Nanga, acquired Rimpa characteristics under Korin's influence and ended in Shijo, changing his name several times on the way. It is as if a thrush had traces of robin, sang like a blackbird and established itself finally among the hawks.

Main streams and general characteristics are easier, the first dividing-point being an allegiance to artistic traditions of Japan, or irresistible fascination with the latest news from China. *Yamato-e* simply meant Japanese picture; its later manifestation as Tosa was typically Japanese—poetic, always recognizable when open scenes, indoor or outdoor, are viewed from above as if roofs were transparent, with opaque drifts of formalized horizontal cloud forming part of the composition.

From China came the oddity of a "north" and a "south" style, unrelated to what anyone supposes those two words to mean. In Chinese art the northern style provided a more clearly defined linear tradition, the southern a greater freedom of expression and impression. Needless to say, the two seldom kept a pure identity. The more impressionist southern school is associated with Nanga, the thinner clarity of the north with Kano. Artists often expressed allegiance to such schools, or to particular masters whose work they admired, by borrowing and using their names—a habit which helps us in following their drift, and confounds us in tracing their lives.

Zen was another mainstream Japanese heritage, which emerged there from China in the twelfth century but developed its local forms of art, descending recognizably through Kano traditions to illustration in books. Zen art in Japan is associated with freely expressive brush-strokes, often with thick dripping brushes, and strong decisive line. We are in immediate trouble: expressive freedom connects with the "southern" Nanga manner from China.

Distinctions in art are no less subtle than in theology: what is meant, for example by "color?" If we think of the rainbow, it came rather late into Japanese books and developed slowly; if we extend it to include a total range of mood in light and shadow, the block-cutters were quick to show their art.

Color printing in Europe is almost as old as the invention of printing. Ugo da Carpi, a master of chiaroscuro in early sixteenth-century Italy, produced powerful results long before comparable attempts began in Japan. European technical advances focused upon the metal cut, one method succeeding another as new effects were mastered. Metal engraving and etching reached Japan towards the end of the eighteenth century; lithography was also a late arrival.

The mastery of color, literal and tonal, occurred in Japan during the eighteenth century, as did its puzzling and parallel abandonment in China. "Two superlative examples of Chinese printed albums," Chibbett wrote,[1] "*Hasshu gafu* (*Pa-chung hau-p'u*), published in China in the 1620s and in Japan in 1671, and *Kaishien gaden* (*Chieh-tzu-yuan hau-chuan, or Mustard Seed Garden Manual*), printed in Japan in 1748 but widely known by the end of the seventeenth century, were received and studied avidly."

They are indeed marvellous works, very different in character, the first black-and-white, chiefly linear, the second treasured as an example of early woodblock

Plate 29. Lan T'ing Pavilion

color-printing in Japan. Yet it should be understood that emulation, not originality, was the motive. These treatises or manuals demonstrated, systematized, formulated methods and conventions by which the most highly respected Chinese artists achieved their effects. One must imagine disciples in Japan, hungry for news of how it ought to be done; out of touch because travel was forbidden, but receiving instruction from such books as these or the occasional presence of a distinguished painter and teacher—Shen Nan Ping for instance—at the trading port of Nagasaki.

Distinctions between painting and illustration are hard to accept, if only because the block-cutters perfected their art of reproducing brush strokes as woodcut. Japan, with no tradition of secular illustration in books, produced tentatively and with total elegance several works from the Saga press (*Saga-bon*) of two artists who used movable type on superb papers at the opening of the Edo period in the seventeenth century (Saga is the name of a province, and of the river which flows through Kyoto). Weeks before writing this I was disturbed by desire for a *Saga-bon* edition, the *Ise Monogatari*, one of the fine and famous early epics, with fine-line illustrations printed on pale mauve and pale green papers, the whole work in two well-filled volumes with original purple covers—so wildly expensive, fortunately, as to lie beyond realms of debate. Elegance and delicacy: one way and another, "north" or "south," these were keys of the kingdom to come.

Color, tempting and beguiling, never of the first importance because line well used can simulate it, grew and spread among Japanese publishers in the second half of the eighteenth century—bright and multiple, or limited artistically to shades of grey and black (*sumi*). These grey-and-black studies, often of bamboo, are perhaps my favorites; the technical distinction was in using more than one block. *The Mustard Seed Garden*, the first part of which was published in late seventeenth-century China, a very rare book in any early Chinese appearance, had wonderful color-printing, after which China abandoned that art—a singular mystery. The first Japanese interpretations of that work also displayed great beauty in wood-block color-prints; in Japan the tradition happily continued.

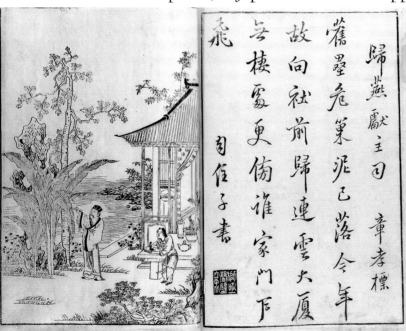

Plate 30. Artist and banana leaf, from Hasshu Gafu

It strikes me therefore as of outstanding interest that an immense scroll known by its ancient title, the *Lan T'ing Preface*, was printed to superb effect using three colors in 1592 in China. Admiration filtered through naturally to Japan [Plate 29]. The whole event became emblematic, not quite mythical, an ideal memory of some fourth-century occasion, celebrated in perfect calligraphy of which no authentic record existed. But the tradition survived, was thought to enshrine it, and was passed down and recorded from one version to another through the centuries. Prince I's irreproachable calligraphy recorded a tranquil scene in which members of the administration, in descending order of rank, sit at intervals by flowing water and among the willow boughs writing poems, while serving-boys float cups of *sake* down the stream on lotus leaves. That was the event, symbol of elegance and civility. In his pavilion overlooking them, served with tea, the prince is seen recording this with spiritual truth, his brush poised over an open scroll—upon which, rather surprisingly, his draped elbow leans.

A tradition of descent, from stone-engraving to rubbing and from place to place, continued for a thousand years. At the end of the sixteenth century this extraordinary scroll, printed from stone or woodblocks (difficult to tell), established it again. Opening with a mighty calligraphic title, the text repeats several times in variant calligraphy the famous Preface, white in the black ground. Similarly reversed into black are the pavilion, trees, rocks, and the poems composed that day. People, stream, waterfall and three geese are all in greenish-grey on white, powerful and startling within the prevailing black.

Plate 31. Poet and fir tree, from Hasshu Gafu

This color-printing from the sixteenth century was duly devoured in Japan. The box which holds my example from 1592 has also a Japanese adaptation of it, a scroll with brush-outline upon fine paper, from that time or very soon after. I have recently seen in a Tokyo bookshop (Gyokueido) an eighteenth-century printed Japanese version in *sumi*—smaller than the original however, missing its poetry. The significance for Japanese books of this scroll, preceding the *Saga-bon* and long before China's *Mustard Seed Garden*, is pleasant to contemplate.

Not long after came the first Chinese edition of *Hasshu Gafu*, which means "Collection of Eight Ming Picture Albums." Though the two have no publishing connection they are from the same vein of thought; for one purpose of the *Lan T'ing* scroll was to keep alive a tradition of perfect calligraphy, and of the *Hasshu Gafu*, to analyze and teach the painting techniques of highly respected Chinese artists. In that sense both were manuals of instruction, looking to high example—and both rose above that purpose, as works of art in their own right.

The first Japanese edition of *Hasshu Gafu* was published in 1671, eight tall volumes, seldom seen. The 1710 reprint is beside me now, trophy from a morning in Jimbo-cho; wholly Chinese in character, printed on soft and sensitive paper [Plates 30–32]. There is no color in this work of delicate line, which also uses and teaches the contrast of solid black. It is a puzzle to know whether the instruction was of more practical use to woodcut craftsmen, over many years, than to painters. Here are the subjects which were to become familiar in so many Japanese books:

plum blossoming from bare branches, symbol of renewal; the graceful forms of bamboo dissected and abstracted, much as Mori Ransai would show in his own manual sixty years later; iris as solid black; dark leaves of chrysanthemum white-veined, and outline petals of the flowers. The season advances in blossom and leaves, with varying attitudes of active birds among them, black or outlined, still or poised for flight, upside-down or watching. Priests and poets, willow and water, the forms of trees and rocks, follow almost as conversation pieces; the occasional

Plate 32. Bird and hops, from Hasshu Gafu

picnic, a book carried out to the poet—and that commonest of presences in Chinese art, the philosopher in his pavilion, small in the landscape, contemplating. One splendidly crazy volume spreads a series of designs for fans across the folds of each leaf, so a double opening shows half the previous fan, and half the next—surely by design, not folly; Ikeno Taiga and others who imitated these fans had to work out the pattern for themselves. The later volumes extend these ideas into more active scenes, compositions, and human presence. A similar convention for fans is repeated in *The Mustard Seed Garden*.

Hasshu Gafu is an enchanting work of the "northern" school, though these divisions are never absolute. If the spirit of experiment is absent, there is no lack of impressionism—how can there be, with shapes abstracted for analysis and outline in common contrast to absolute black? It came to Japan as one sort of influence: the people, clothes, horses and conventions of drawing are Chinese. What is the distinction between humility and ambition, in passionately needing the fashion of high example? Technically the block-cutters were not experimenting: here is no attempt at texture, or gradation of light and dark through slightly varied pressure on inking levels of the surface. Nothing of comparable sophistication had been known in Japan before.

Painters became engaged upon the work itself, rather than educational demonstration of how it was accomplished. Printers had the double task of explaining and performing, and followed it for most of two centuries. In the mid-eighteenth century, *The Mustard Seed Garden*, Japanese version of a Chinese exemplar, advanced both endeavors dramatically. Those ten volumes, produced as two works in 1748

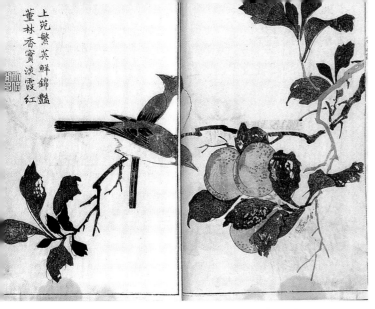

Plate 33. *Bird and plums, from* The Mustard Seed Garden

and 1756, provided a pattern in decorum and an artistic achievement which held its ideal place among publishers and designers into the Meiji period. Within it was equal scope for imitation of the fashionable and exploration of the new. Painters could combine respect with adventure in a single work; publishers and blockmakers divided these functions through their several volumes [Plates 33–37].

Thus the 1748 *Mustard Seed Garden*, copying the Chinese edition, devoted the first of five volumes to explanatory text in elegant Chinese calligraphy and, through all this work, on fine soft paper. The next demonstrates, as had the *Hasshu Gafu*, forms of flower, leaf, branch. Volume Three brings a poetic surprise: color-printing in all these subjects in shades of pink, orange, green, brown, grey. Half a dozen blocks are used across the double-page opening, often with no outline drawing or merely casual register. A new book art is at once produced: wholly different from Western use of color in books or prints; characterized by poetry of light, in color and texture. One surprising achievement was a grained appearance in the inking, to be developed and enjoyed by generations of Japanese block-cutters after

Plate 34. *From* The Mustard Seed Garden

the publication of these books—though to this day nobody quite knows how it was done. Ink, pressure, wood surface were all reduced perhaps, but the subtle mixture is forgotten.

On it goes through Volume Four, which has one masterpiece of snow on pink

Plate 35. *Snow on blossom, from* The Mustard Seed Garden

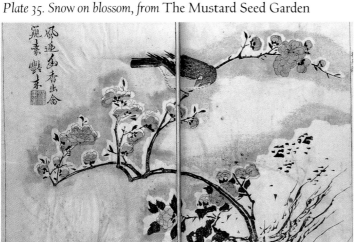

blossom against a grey hint of winter [Plate 35], suggesting long maturity rather than early experiment. The fifth volume returns to outline demonstration of figure sketches, the sixth similarly to animals, roofs and boats. The whole work in its yellow covers becomes a rising and falling graph in its scope—one thinks of Shakespeare's sonnet,

Desiring this man's art and that man's scope.

I believe it would be correct to say that tones in the two volumes of color were not later to be repeated, though they were attempted—perhaps because the quality of paper used in 1748 was exceptional. Pinks and yellows, fugitive when exposed but safe in a book, give to this work a Chinese feeling which will not reappear.

It seems to me that everything in the second publication (1756, embossed grey covers), was *almost* as good but not quite; the paper a little less refined and color, when it comes, less accomplished. But it is a splendid event closely following in design the original Chinese work. Again the first volume is text; the next two analyze in outline the forms of tree, rock, mountain, as Chinese painters abstracted and expressed them—influential albums of reference. Volume Four continues thus through landscape, wave and waterfall, breaking half-way into demonstrations with color—so differing from the earlier work that one could suppose another group of artists and painters prepared them. Here are larger areas of color, wider use of grey. The ability to create texture within solid is present again; yellow and pink occur, as does snow on the mountain trees. This has the appearance of an earlier, more primitive endeavor than the other; but that cannot have been so.[2] The fifth and final volume combines effects which had been shown before, within arcs and circles of fans across the double pages.

An unusual sophistication in binding this second series is the presence of a blank leaf within each folded page. Most Japanese

Plate 36. From The Mustard Seed Garden, 1756

books show folds at the outer edge, giving the appearance of leaves uncut. The blank leaf was inserted to make the paper more opaque and avoid show-through. I have seen several later instances of this helpful but difficult practice, or various papers inserted with the same purpose by an earlier owner of the book. Ginko leaves are sometimes there too—used as bookmarks perhaps, or souvenirs of a shady place where the volume was enjoyed.

Particular characteristics of these two works, *Hasshu Gafu* and *The Mustard Seed Garden*, were developed and extended by artists and printers through all the great period of illustrated books. The range of Chinese styles was there; they had only to choose. *Hasshu Gafu*, concerned more with method than inspiration, was of the "northern" school; that appeared too in *The Mustard Seed Garden*, along with a technical courage and formal daring—especially in the rocks and mountains of 1756—which spanned the "southern" Nanga school.

Advances towards color in the history of printing are like advances towards accuracy; both are concepts difficult to define. If the late eighteenth century brought assured color-printing, the way had been cleared by command of texture in black and grey. The range was from elegant discipline to a wild impressionism.

Black-and-grey (*sumi*) spanned them all, arriving at the fine and famous *Hundred Views of Mount Fuji* by Hokusai, a work which

Plate 37. From The Mustard Seed Garden, 1756

defies definition or the limits of one "school." Those schools in Japanese art history become a dominating nuisance, taking one's attention from the work; yet they existed so formally that a painter might be expelled if his style changed. Such artists as Hokusai and Yamaguchi Soken could work in several styles; then they add to our confusion by using a variety of names. Look up, for example, the second Kunisada, a prolific artist through the late Edo period, in the dictionary of Japanese artists, and this is what you find:

> Kunisada II (1823–80). N. Utagawa (originally Takenouchi) Munehisa. F.N.: Masakichi; later, Seitaro. Go: Baido, Horaisha, Ichijusai, Ichiyosai, Kochoro, Kunimasa III, Kunisada, Toyokuni IV. Biog: Ukiyo-e printmaker. Pupil of Kunisada. At first signed his prints Baido Kunimasa III or Kunimasa, pupil of Kochoro; in 1846 married his master's daughter, took go of Kunisada II and used with it the go of Kochoro and Ichijusai. About 1870, after Kunisada's death, began to use go of Toyokuni IV.

From old Zen traditions, as has been mentioned, came a style of emphatic line-drawing associated with generations of Kano artists who successively took that name with their own, creating a "school." Moronobu in the seventeenth century was an illustrator and painter in this manner. Books in which his flowing designs appeared are admired for exploring a style which was not imitated from Chinese models and made its influence felt. Those books (less hard to find now than impossible to afford) were popular productions, not printed on exquisite papers or patterned with mica-dust, as had been the finest volumes issued by Koetsu and Soan years before at Saga.

Throughout the early eighteenth century, black-line woodcuts were commonly used to illustrate *Noh* plays and popular tales. Picture-books, fortunately for us, were enjoyed in Japan; we may enjoy them now, without needing the language. Styles prevailed and continued. Here is a rare work from 1734, *Ehon Yoroi Sakura*, which means "Picture Book: Armor of Cherry." The *Ehon* or picture-book was a venerable tradition; these heroic and mythic warriors are interpreted in a style familiar from paintings of an earlier day—epic scrolls that pre-date the Tokugawa era, sixteenth century or before. Powerful line, strong action, formal horseman-ship, cruel force—all are translat-ed with assurance into the line and solid black associated with Kano artists. Of course we are in trouble at once from that sugges-tion, for the patterns of wave and armor bring to mind another artist, Korin, who died in 1716 and inspired a different school called Rimpa, its name derived from the second syllable of his.

Plate 38. Lotus bud, from Morikuni's Umpitsu Soga

But Settei, who lived a little later, with whom this anonymous book of warriors has been associated,[3] is remembered as a Kano artist.

This leads us towards a pioneering work in three volumes: *Umpitsu Soga*, issued in 1749, by another Kano artist, Tachibana Morikuni [Plate 38]. As the book's subject was coarse-brush technique in painting (another in the long line of manuals which became works of art), his block-cutters needed to find ways of suggesting texture, transcending line. This they did with daring and success. Just how the slithering half-filled paint-brush, conveying its poetry of branch and foliage, could be transferred to black line-block remains mysterious, but so it was, a translation of textured mass in woodblock print. The granular effect recalls aquatint, mezzotint, anything but woodcut as Europe ever knew it.

Such is the character throughout this book, of wildlife, water and natural scene. Flowers become flames, nothing is static; this was impressionism, of horses or a hanging wisteria, in compositions which still astonish; always with the self-effacing purpose of demonstrating brush-techniques. One admires the artist in it—but also, equally, the block-cutter. Morikuni's book, appearing just after his death, was contemporary with the Japanese *Mustard Seed Garden*. Several artists in their books of illustration explored styles and techniques thus exposed.

An artist's *go* was the pseudonym by which he chose to be known. Mokyo Tatebe, painter and monk, wrote several kinds of poetry. As *haiku* author he took the name Ryotai; as scholar accomplished in a form of Japanese lyric called *waka* his name was Ayata or Ayatazi; as artist he was called Kanyosai. "It is said that he often astonished people with his genius and eccentricity,"[4] leaving his patron after a sharp quarrel, becoming a monk at the Kofuku-ji in Kyoto. His tutor in Japanese classic literature was his wife. He died at the age of fifty-six in 1774.

Following the convention of the teaching manual but extending it as his work of art, towards the end of his life he issued the *Kenshi Gaen* or "Painting Garden" of Master Tatebe. Of these three volumes the first opens in a style most recognizably Chinese as in *Hasshu Gafu*, departing at once to show such impressionist textures as appeared in Morikuni's *Umpitsu Soga*. Volume Two starts with a quietly printed double page, continuing with poetic *sumi* scenes of rock, water and snow; one double-page shows an idyllic meeting of three friends below cliffs and trees by the sea, while a couple of servants prepare tea and food. The final volume is filled with powerful portraits of fish.

Kanyosai was perhaps most inventive in *Mokyo Wakan Zatsuga* ("Miscellaneous Japanese and Chinese Drawings by Mokyo") where black arrangements across the double openings, of plants, scenery and animals, retain their power to astonish. His kindly view of animals was never sentimental. A stooping elephant is sometimes reproduced, but I choose the startling design of two white rabbits on the black and textured ground [Plate 39]. To leap ahead to a book and artist not yet mentioned, it is intriguing to compare Kanyosai's snail on a banana leaf with the treatment Utamaro gave to a similar subject [Plate 40].

Plate 39 (following pages). Kanyosai: Rabbits, from Mokyo Wakan Zatsuga   63

Two volumes posthumously published, the *Kanga Shinan Nihen* ("Guide to Chinese Painting"), again within a convention but extending beyond it, are memorable for studies of water-irises, their untidy leaves straying across both pages. Kawamura Bumpo, among the finest book-artists in this gentle tradition, paid tribute in giving his own comparable work the same title, "second series."

Little is known of Mori Ransai, a Nagasaki artist, and there are confusing collations of *Ransai Gafu* by which he is remembered [Plate 41]. The date was 1801 or perhaps much earlier (he died in 1802); it may have been in four volumes, or three series of four. Those which I can examine—studies in painting, bamboo leaves and stems—are sufficiently extraordinary to defy neglect. In Japan bamboo grows as thick straight poles, green when young, bending in the wind or under a weight of snow. This

Plate 40. Kanyosai: Snail, *from* Mokyo Wakan Zatsuga

gafu or manual of instruction advances from abstract form to the greatest grace of tone, design and occasional color-printing. Snow, grey days, the rustle of leaves are all suggested. The block-cutters managed total control of their art.

Better known than the *Ransai Gafu*, earlier and offering experiments in color-printing, was the *So Shiseki Gafu* of 1765. This artist, who also used several other names, admired Chinese painting but spent his time in Edo rather than Nagasaki. It is indeed an admirable work of varied experiment through three volumes, displaying shades, tones, and the unusual technique of colors applied *à la poupée*—one block inked with several colors like a painting, all printed at once instead of from separate blocks for each ink. Credit was given—a rare event—to the two block-cutters, Tanaka Heibei and Tanaka Chushichi. The range is impressive, from fine-line imitation of Chinese "northern" style to reproductions of the artist's own Nanga paintings. Keeping in mind its date, the block-cutters' names and the coloring, this may strike first as a technical achievement. His own work in several double pages of Volume Three is the best.

Yamaguchi Soken is an example of the complexity of art-history in Japan if one's focus rests upon "schools"—but that would be true of Millais, who began as a Pre-

Raphaelite and became successfully academic. Soken was, we read, "considered one of the ten most notable pupils of Okyo;" and of Okyo we read that he "founded the Maruyama school, in which his style, a combination of Muromachi *suiboku* and close, accurate observation of nature, was continued." Well, *suiboku* was the Zen style of landscape art, line-drawing with India ink. This has been identified with "an unprecedented abandon" which must lie far from Okyo's "sketchbooks with detailed studies of nature."

Japanese artists seem sometimes to be have been like versatile actors who could throw themselves into any part they chose to perform. Hanging on the wall opposite me is a painted scroll by Soken in the Ukiyo-e manner, young woman with a small dog, her patterned green kimono drawn in tightly, a study in controlled neatness. On the table are four books by Soken, of which two belong to that vein of textured impressionism descending from Morikuni. We shall look at the others later.

Soken was a black-and-white artist, line and grain and grey, who lived in Kyoto and died there in 1818, aged sixty. The three volumes of *Soken Gafu, Soka No bu* ("Album of Drawings by Soken, Plant Part") appeared in 1806; a work which inspired Jack Hillier to write that "his prints reach down to depths of our being with reactions on our part that cannot be rationalized." Among all the wandering expressions of freedom

Plate 41. Bamboo, from Ransai Gafu, Volume 1

in design across two pages, none known to me is more varied and admirable than this. Experiment extends from texture and arrangement to black lines upon pale grey, or grey with no black, and minimal use of outline blocks. This most gentle book plays once with pale blue in the grey, and two lines of red.

One other work I find enchanting, though it earns less praise from Hillier, is *Soken Sansui Gafu* ("A Book of Landscape Drawings by Soken") which appeared in 1818, the year of his death [Plate 42]. Less experimental than the last, this is a poetic exhibition of landscape, snow, water, moonlight, in tones of grey and black. Again we know the name of the woodcut artist, Inoue Jihei. "*Très bon tirage,*" an enthusiastic owner wrote in the fly-leaf of this copy, and I would agree.

The total divide between the use and achievements of texture in Japan and Europe was never clearer than in these *sumi* books. As is often explained, effects of light and shade in Western prints were achieved by cross-hatching, until the invention of mezzotint (which means half-tone) in the third quarter of the seventeenth century. Mezzotint provided gradation of shading, dark to light, but its use was wholly different; a mezzotint begins black all over, and the engraver scrapes down for lighter areas. Aquatint, with resin-dust covering the copper plate, was printed from more and less deeply etched areas. Textured woodcut in Japan almost always started with white and used it, especially in half-suggested mists, waves, snow and distance. The interest, often as not, was in pale grey and emptiness.

Plate 42. Soken: from Soken Sansui Gafu, *1818. "In the bleak midwinter."*

1. Page 209
2. Since writing the above, I have understood that the later (1756) Japanese volumes faithfully reproduce the earlier (1679) Chinese volumes.
3. Jack Hillier, rejecting other attributions, has called it "Proto-Settei."
4. Mitchell, Page 85

CHAPTER SIX
ILLUSTRATED BOOKS II

THE experience of looking through these books of prints and writing about them recalls a term at my prep school when the task was to prepare and deliver a lecture, on any subject, and I airily chose The National Gallery, nothing less, having no notion of large monographs written on every artist exhibited there. After my talk the headmaster, reasonably polite, said, "You can't *describe* a *picture.*" His simple truth, not aimed at my own failure particularly, remains.

To avoid a cascade of poetic epithet it may be well to change direction, from early romanticism of black-and-grey, to a vein of social realism which descends from the strong-line Kano artists and from Zen, but looks with close good humor upon the unfashionable and everyday, at life and crowds in cities. A passage from the description of Ukiyo-e ("the floating world"), in the late seventeenth century, mentioned those artists as "diverting ourselves just in floating, floating, caring not a whit for the pauperism staring us in the face. . ." I am not now considering Ukiyo-e, but there was a form of Shijo art which cared very much for pauperism staring it in the face; which stared back with sympathetic humor, finding the poetry of human incident no less observable than blossoms and mountains.

Shijo was, and still is, a street and district in Kyoto; it used to be an artists' quarter as Hampstead was once, or "The Village" in New York, where writers gathered with their painter friends to draw, drink, produce their poems. They formed, it is said, groups or clubs. They are remembered for expressive pictures of

Plate 43. Soken: Calling them in to the restaurant, from Yamato Jimbutsu Gafu, II, 1804

birds and plants, but more quickly recognizable are studies of street life, shops, the bath-house, chaotic children—the working rather than the floating moment. Strong line characterized this, and to some extent it was the art of caricature; yet their perception seldom descended to satire. The social realism of observed instants across two pages, recorded as impressions, declared a photographer's eye, very far from the easy precision of photography. Distortion—Roger Fry's "significant distortion"—was the heart of it.

Examples of these Shijo books cross from black to color almost before one notices; that was not their essence, either way. They began to proliferate at the close of the eighteenth century, and one could take up the thread with Soken's *Yamato Jimbutsu Gafu* ("Album of Japanese Figure Drawings") published in two three-volume groups, 1800 and 1804 [Plate 43]. Each volume of the first series introduces itself with a tree; of the second, with clever figure studies: in mass and space, no line. After those, perceptions of life—sleazy now and then, fun-loving, fashionless. These are sketch books from life, perceptions, compositions: priests and processions, restaurants, work, the bath-house; they have no text.

Ki Baitai's two volumes from a few years before should be mentioned among the black-and-whites: *Kyuro Gafu* ("Book of Drawings by Kyuro"). These woodcuts of his soft-line drawings, page by page, the arrangement never accidental, less street-wise than Soken's work, come from the same realm of observation. One version of this book had *haiku* poems, which always formed part of the visual as well as the literary adornment; the other version has no text. This often happens—like coffee and milk, acceptable with or without.

I have two particular favorites in this kind: Kawamura Kiho's *Kafuku Nimpitsu* ("The Ups and Downs of Life Represented"), 1809 [Plate 44], and Aikawa Minwa's *Manga Hyaku-Jo* ("Sketches of a Hundred Women"), 1814 [Plate 45]. Kiho, pupil and adopted son of Bumpo whose gently colored books we shall look at later, lived in Kyoto close to fellow Shijo artists; his lyrical *Gafu* in the style of Bumpo, issued fifteen years later, was very different from this humorous record of chaos. In

Plate 44. Kiho: Domestic business, from Kafuku Nimpitsu

black-and-grey, with pale pink added occasionally, and using thick decisive line, we see domestic quarrels, lack of ceremony, pipes smoked, nits picked, slatternly clothes, a traditional Japan where custom held its place but poverty ruled the style. Here was no occasion for decorum; stooping laborers expose bare bottoms, children scrap while their father seems to shout "Shut up, the lot of you." Violence and confusion prevail, on the whole, in disorder of dress and face at a far end of the spectrum from Ukiyo-e, courtly conduct, samurai.

Minwa has been described as a minor artist, but his range took him from this precious survey of women's lives to an adaptation of Korin's *Gashiki* or book of drawing methods, in entirely different style. We can only be grateful for his record in a hundred prints, social realism with abundant life, of the women's world in old Japan—elegant occasionally, more often hard-working, domestic, professional;

Plate 45. Minwa: Domestic bath, from Manga Hyaku-jo, 1814

told truly, it seems, using the manner of conversational idiom and the blockmaker's technique of black-and-grey with pale pink. So, across the double pages they talk: spinning, weaving, dyeing, making

71

up kimonos, planting rice, picking tea, living domestically; preparing rice-cakes, dragging a screaming child, packing fans, bathing; only once we see the highly born, who contemplates the moon from her balcony. On fine soft paper and with the skills of caricature (as when an old woman sucks twine, with twisted face, to thread her needle) this is a restful book to leaf through, crossing social frontiers.

An Osaka album in this kind from 1814, the *Gafu* of Sato Suiseki, using pale colors on thin brownish paper, gives a surprising repose in coarse-line satirical sketches of working life—people singly or in small groups, big-headed. These are action studies, even when the pressed-down hand and hunched shoulders of a child at his lesson show his boredom. It is a famous book, much praised: glass-blower, gardeners, priests (smug and portly), bookbinders at their press, generally studies of couples and small groups working. The mood conveyed is not of noise or chaos but the tranquillity of labor.

Very different is the *Nantei Gafu*, 1804, black-and-white impressions of street scenes and tumult, Japanese ribaldry [Plate 46]. This restless book of crowds and

parties has a few moments of moderate peace, but most of its people are shouting, shifting, drunk; supper and music suggest more fidget than peace; a procession of novices behind their priest is rumbustious rather than religious. Nishimura Nantei, with a rare use of strong sketch-lines satirically, belongs—in these three volumes anyway—among the realists and recorders.

For a bridge from one kind of book to another, leading towards the use of more blocks for color-printing, one may look at the work of Onishi

Plate 46. From Nantei Gafu, 1804. *"Relative peace in the kitchen."*

Chinnen, who produced two brilliant and contrasting albums. Chinnen lived in Tokyo (Edo), a samurai "attached to the Tokugawa government" we are told, "in charge of the rice granaries." It sounds like a lucrative position. He died in 1851 at the age of fifty-nine.

Azuma No Teburi ("Customs of the Eastern Capital, Scenes of the Great Peace"), 1829, in the manner and mood of those several described above, suggests this samurai had a sympathetic understanding of the people he governed [Plate 47]. In pale colors on soft paper it explores across double pages the festivals and happenings and domesticities which caught his eye. One can only feel pleased to know that Chinnen, controller of the granaries, observed an old man, spectacled, closely reading as a maid massages his back and his wife stoops with lighted taper to cope with bugs on her toes; a couple of fashionable ladies on a winter walk through snow, by a lake, followed by two servants with picnic gear; an elderly father with his infant and wife,

Plate 47. Chinnen: from Azuma No Teburi, 1829. Domestic scene

all naked by their bathtubs; or the basket-makers, several sorts of pedlar, children spinning tops, potters, musicians. This quiet work in free line, undisciplined, records scenes of calm and noise in a kindly spirit.

*   *   *   *   *

A FEW reflections about color, before advancing into some books whose reputation and attraction owe much to its use. I choose to view them in three groups: the lightly colored, the deeply colored, and Ukiyo-e—spending least time on the last which have been most thoroughly considered, are best known and widely popular.

As to pale and dark, that too is matter for controversy. We used to be told, of Morris curtains and fabrics, that vegetable dyes were the source of their beauty; no chemicals or composites for him. Those who are acquainted with them know how they faded in sunlight, like water-color drawings. I was educated in the same rules for Japanese prints: avoid the vulgarity of later taste, the chemical colors. It ruled out some very jolly examples, and I followed advice.

That strikes me as doubtful guidance, as do most fashionable customs in collecting. In Tokyo last month I was much tempted by a series of large prints in the form of a book, on green-bordered paper, by Toyokuni III, a name adopted late in his career by Kunisada I. The date was 1859; color, strong greens and reds; the subject, geishas in their kimonos. Even the bookseller conveyed to me—though not he but the price deterred—that I was in bad taste admiring them. "His early prints his best," says the work of reference, "with his work growing coarse and violent in obedience to popular 19th-century taste and much of it hastily designed, overcolored, badly printed."

I regret leaving them there. Here is a smaller album of paintings on silk, in Chinese style, by a Japanese artist called Taizan, from the 1790s [Plate 48]. They have similar greens and the same crowded coloring of those tasteless Kunisada prints. Follow your spirit, must be the advice to any collector; don't do as you are told. That the taste for strong colors was popular is not against them:

Plate 48. From an album of paintings on silk by Taizan, circa 1790

the most highly prized actor-prints by Sharaku were so. None of the blockmaker's art, nor the printer's, was in decline. As an example of this decadent color I reproduce an illustration from one of Kunisada's wittily erotic interpretations of Genji's courtly love, all stops pulled out for an organ-blast of color printing [Plates 49–50].

Indeed, those skills lived through the first half of this century. I have been examining an almost unknown book, two volumes in Shijo style produced in 1918: Toshu's *Seso Hyakushi* ("One Hundred Forms of Everyday Life"). Tamate Toshu was a little-known artist who died in 1871 at the age of seventy-six; a publisher decided, four decades later, that a scroll of his painted studies deserved to be printed. These scenes of varied cultural activity reproduce the artist's water-color drawings by colored woodblocks of such deceptive excellence of shading and brush-stroke that a glass was needed to detect the method. "This style of facsimile color-printing is a feature of the Taisho period books," wrote Jack Hillier in a descriptive analysis he most kindly provided for me. The names of printer and block-cutter appear in the colophon.

It must be accepted that such works as this were harder for both printer and blockmaker to manage than even the most complex Ukiyo-e prints, where flat colors simply needed, once a system for perfect register was managed, a variable number of blocks and impressions.

No doubt the methods varied also. When two shades of color crossed one area there was no need for two blocks; one could be wiped clean and inked appropriately for the next printing. The received version, that each tone meant another block, may not always be right.

Whatever the ethics and aesthetics of color, only from the darkness of books can we see what was intended.

*   *   *   *   *

COLOR-PRINTING advanced slowly into Shijo books, pale pinks and greens added to grey and black. Several artists in this pale-color idiom may be viewed together as a convenient group; the more brilliant and diverse tones of Ukiyo-e books and prints, in full vogue by the close of the eighteenth century, were not for them. Kawamura Bumpo, a Kyoto artist and poet, prolific as a painter and popular in his books, died at the age of forty-two in 1821; so his working life spanned the best Shijo period, or partly caused it.

Several volumes of his *Gafu* from early in the century [Plate 51] when he was in his twenties, show the high reputation he quickly achieved; a peony, in flower and leaf, vine with fruit, have their place, but the greater fascination was commonly with winter: snowy landscape, bare trees, snow on bamboo, and the symbolic miracle of flowers—plum, magnolia—from leafless twigs. If one example were taken from this work, I would choose the living solidity of magnolia rising like a graph of summer across two pages, one flower out, two buds like candle flames, a bee flying in; all heavy black except for two smears of pink at the center of the flower and edge of a petal. In the apparently casual, nothing was casual. High summer—even the advance of spring—seems to have moved these artists less. Bumpo's figure-studies, two or three to a page, give more space for appreciation than the crowded little people in Hokusai's *Manga*.

Plate 49. Kunisada's parody of Genji: covers, wrapper and box   *Plate 50 (following pages). From Kunisada's parody of Genji*

五十四帖
三

Pale coloring, snow, skies overcast, and the several conventions (far from botanical) by which Chinese artists conveyed differing forms of trees, dominate Bumpo's four volumes recording his native Kyoto, *Teito Gakei Ichiran* ("Sights of the Imperial

Capital"). The album he shared with another artist, Nangaku, belongs properly in the vein of social realism mentioned before: *Kaido Kyoka Awase* ("Comparison of Kyoka Poems on the Highway"), 1811. *Kyoka*, light verse, far removed from those senior ministers gathered by the river to pass their poems and drink *sake* as recorded in the Lan T'ing scroll, sometimes accompanied these scenes of humble life on the highway, or they were omitted. This again overlaps with illustra-

Plate 51. Bumpo Gafu, 1st series: "Rising like a graph of summer..."

tions and broadsheets where related poems contributed to the page design. This book of activity and rest, mountains and streets, from rain and the snowy highway to a man passing the time chatting, as he leans over the barrier, with women naked at their bath, in unexpected ways brings modern Japan to mind; for in lives which may strike us as restrictive and tough, good humor prevailed over bad temper. Bumpo gives enough evidence that hard work and heavy weight in the rain provided more fun than complaint.

Kanyosai's *Kanga Shinan Nihen* ("Guide to Chinese Painting") was mentioned earlier; Bumpo expressed homage by giving his three volumes in 1811 the same title, "second series" [Plate 52]. The second and third volumes rise far beyond instruction, to his own pale poetry of landscape and form; his waterfall studies disappear into the abstract.

Sansui Gafu ("Album of Landscapes") appeared in Kyoto three years after Bumpo's death, the publisher's tribute in producing, rather more luxuriously than before, thirty paintings from his last period. Four colors were used, always pale; the yellow covers are decorated with bamboo leaves.

Plate 52. Bumpo, Kanga Shinan Nihen: Waterfall study

A book close to Bumpo's spirit is the *Kiho Gafu* ("Book of Drawings by Kiho") of 1827 [Plate 53]; indeed, Kawamura Kiho, a year older than Bumpo and living until 1852, was his adopted son—which really means his acknowledged disciple. A particular attraction of this work, in its blue covers with patterns of waves in mica, is a group of three prints spread through it of people reading: one

Plate 53. Kiho Gafu, 1827: Reading, while he binds a sheaf...

binds his sheaf of rice, standing to press with his foot, looking at an open book on the ground beyond it; another, dressed handsomely, reads one volume by the glow of some form of lamp bundled and suspended, four other volumes beside him in their *chitsu*; the third, comfortably robed and younger, leans on a pile of books and reads by the light of the moon. I cannot approve the way these last two hold their books, rolled back in one hand like a newspaper; if this volume had been so handled, it would not have survived thus. This varied work of pale coloring includes one sympathetic print of an old man contemplating the plants in his nursery.

In similar spirit, perhaps even more highly accomplished, is the *Koshu Gafu* ("Book

of Drawings by Koshu") first issued in 1812 [Plate 54]. Hatta Koshu lived from 1760 to 1822 in Kyoto, entirely a Shijo artist as were Bumpo and Kiho. Here again is an old man reading, as he rests against the sheaf of rice. Koshu managed magically living designs of a persimmon blossom and wisteria wandering over the pages like an insect, helped equally by the block-cutter

Plate 54. From Koshu Gafu, 1812: The potter at his wheel

who understood brush-strokes. In this most diverse gathering one notices the alertness of a bird, echoed by a similar spirit in two buds rising from grass and unfolding opposite; and a woodpecker totally absorbed by life in the tree-bark, a study of grey-black with pink in his feathers and the autumn maple leaves.

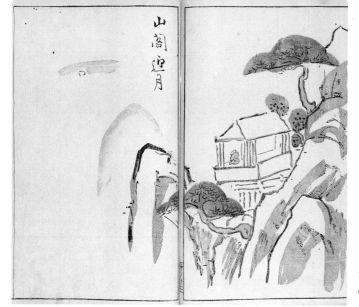

Plate 55. From Taigado Gafo, 1804: The poet in his pavilion

If one were to choose a single work to display the spirit of Shijo it could be *Keijo Gaen* ("Album of Pictures by Kyoto Artists"), 1814, because the printing and coloring on the soft paper are most beautiful and some of the best contributed to this—among them Goshun, Soken, Chikudo, Toyo, Keibun, Toyoshiko, Kiho, Nangaku. Nothing in it is finer than the first two subjects: by Matsumura Goshun, of a sailing barge with its load of three large black-and-grey *daikon*,¹ with just a ripple of water spilling to the empty right-hand page; and Soken's observation (also *sumi* except for a little blue and orange on the bird's head), of a crane crouching to end its flight in the reeds.

This small group (as in any anthology, though it should continue forever) may close with some mention of two favorite books, both Chinese or Nanga or "southern" or impressionist in manner, very different in character: *Kyochusan* ("Imagined Mountains") by Bosai, and the *Taigado Gafo* ("Taigado's Pictorial Methods") of 1804 [Plate 55]. They belong by pale coloring; Kameda Bosai's style is not too far away, but here is no common life from the street, just boatmen in the distance or philosophers viewing the scene, small, dwarfed. It is a book of hints and suggestions of form, printed on softest paper.

Ikeno Taiga (or Taigado) died in 1776, long before his *Gafo* was produced. He worked to spread the Nanga influence in Japan, and was known also as calligrapher, poet and mountaineer. If such artists as Chinnen influenced Cezanne, Taiga had a manifest effect upon German Expressionists. If his defiantly mannered, formalized mountains, trees, rice-fields made a statement, it was elegantly phrased. Shades of black and grey were enough, but color contributed smudges for trunk and tree and sky. I cannot judge whether the difference or the excellence of Taiga has contributed more to his reputation.

Plate 56. Double page from Meika Gafu, 1814

Pale and restricted coloring distinguishes a delicate collection of prints by a group of artists, published in 1814, *Meika Gafu* ("Book of Drawings by Celebrated Artists") [Plate 56]. As the artists combined in this album to represent several styles of Chinese

80

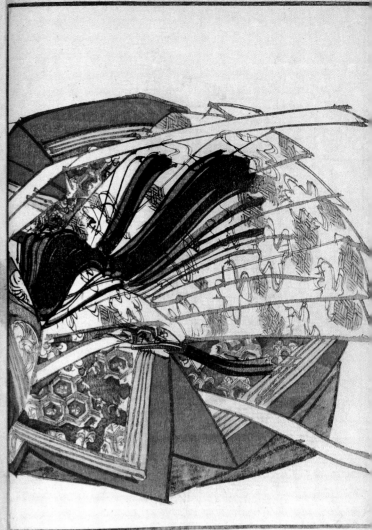

Plate 57. From Chinnen, Sonan Gafu, 1834: Girl calligrapher

painting, it is not surprising to find Taiga among them. All the skills and talents are there, "northern" and Nanga, from precise line to expressionist smudge, from a large and famous frog to the small boy wrapped against winter, folded parasol under one arm and a branch of flowering plum over the other shoulder; bamboo and birds of course, hill and stream, Kitao Masayoshi's observation of an infant rolling a large snowball across a sky so pale it can barely be seen. The contrast between Taigado's mountains and the priest riding his ox (emblem of self-command), the latter in thin Chinese line, is extreme.

A use of strong color, and more of it, is neither wonderful nor decadent, merely historic; never more beautifully shown perhaps than in Onishi Chinnen's *Sonan Gafu* ("Book of Drawings by Sonan"), 1834, published in Tokyo [Plate 57]. Sonan was of course Chinnen, the name he chose to use. A satisfactory copy of this book is beyond realms of ordinary praise: paper, color, printing are wonderful; subjects travel from street-observation (as in Chinnen's *Azuma no Teburi* noticed above) to flower and bird prints, turtles (*au naturel* or as parodies of archery), a boating picnic, the tub-maker, and several free-drawn compositions of women and their accom-

CHAPTER SIX: ILLUSTRATED BOOKS II   81

plishments (painting, calligraphy, music, or just feeding ducks). Hillier chose a double-page of trees from this book, for both jackets of his own. As many of my favorites in coloring, design and subject are here I cannot choose one above another; my desert-island volume would be the *Sonan Gafu*.

The danger in color was descent from art into prettiness, ornament, suburbia. Osaka artist Nishiyama Kan'ei, who died in 1897, produced an admirable *Gafu* in 1886, height of the Meiji period, most of the good traditions still present; wholly a Japanese book but missing the magic. When color printing arrives at its peak the need for experiment vanishes. Viewed in any exhibition, this attracts and stuns. A near-contemporary who lived until 1918, Watanabe Seitei, popular now in Japan, suffered the same problem of working at the close of a period, in an old manner which had been perfected half a century before his time. He and his printers could do it, but one thinks of hotel wall-paper. It is an unfair comment on passages of effective poetry, but Seitei was among those Japanese artists who travelled to Paris and swallowed the influences they found.

This is matter for debate, in both places. Some Japanese artists—Tsukuji Fujita, Gyosai Kyosai—remained capable of both voices, like actors and ventriloquists. In the great

Fujita collection exhibited permanently at Akita in northern Honshu one sees a vast screen and many paintings in Fujita's own idiom, along with Parisian drawings, portraits, notebooks. Kyosai studied local and foreign artists, commented and composed in their many styles, publishing a curious work of demonstration with Japanese and English text block-printed, the *Kyosai Gaden*, in 1887. But vital essence evaporates from the last phase of a tradition. Kyosai laid down rules for students:

"As painting is the art of copying several objects with their different shapes. . ." he begins; wisely, a little later, "Though picture must be copied like the natural growth of all things, yet it lacks the taste and feeling by resembling the real things." Perhaps the worry for a Western viewer of Japanese paintings from the early years of this century is that they too closely resembled fashionable Europe; and that seems more like failure than achievement.

There are finer and earlier matters to view before finishing. Korin, using about a dozen names, is remembered as a designer-painter, rejoicing in rhythm more than precision, waves and motion rather than shape. The second syllable of his Korin name gave a label to his followers, the Rimpa school. He lived from 1658 to 1716, an admirer of Koetsu and Soan who printed the *Saga-bon* books. Korin's style appears much later in the work of artists who studied him, most notably Hoitsu and Minwa.

Sakai Hoitsu, of aristocratic Edo birth, connected himself with several groups or schools of painters before settling on Rimpa. In 1797, not yet forty, he became a Buddhist priest, and "spent the last 21 years of his life in seclusion, painting and studying the life and works of Korin." Among the most beautiful books known to me is his *Oson Gafu* of 1817 (Oson being one of his many names). The Rimpa theme of waves announces itself at once, mica-printed on the

Plate 58. Hoitsu: from Oson Gafu, *1817*

blue covers. Two famous openings of the book show a solid tea-bowl in shades of black, beside an equally solid white camellia, its leaves black like the pot, grey stem and outline, only a little yellow within the flower [Plate 58]; and a bush of yellow starry flowers at the edge of water where unreal waves and ripples are printed silver. More obvious but not less excellent is a large iris leaning from its leaves to the right-hand page, of such purple as would have faded from existence if much exposed; a splash of wave and spray, dramatic as Hokusai's; snow melting in blue streaks down the side of Fuji; and at intervals through this book flower-and-branch designs delicately contrived without use of outline. Hoitsu was responsible also for two volumes in simple tribute to Korin, *Korin Hyakuzu* ("One Hundred Sketches by Korin"), 1815 and 1826; a long black-and-white series where waves and irises are again prominent, on fans and screens and the covers of both volumes. It is most probable that such iris designs descended to Beardsley from Korin via Hoitsu.

Minwa, whose record of women's days in old Japan was mentioned earlier, produced his *Korin Gashiki* ("Drawing Methods of Korin") in 1818—an unfindable edition, reprinted three years later. This is an admirable color-representation of the style in which fact often gives way to shape and design, as on papers and fabrics. Nakamura Hochu, another Rimpa painter, had taken this manner to wonderful extremes in a hopelessly rare work in two volumes, *Korin Gafu* of 1802. These art nouveau shapes still astonish, when viewed in a Meiji period reprint. Though nobody in his senses desires reprints or facsimiles, nowhere were they closer in spirit to the real

Plate 59. Masayoshi: from Sansui Ryakuga-Shiki, 1800

thing than in Japan, with skills and techniques unchanging, woodcut and paper, inking, printing. As the entire process had always meant copying, this is a far cry from, say, the photogravure of a Roxburghe Club book.

These notes on certain kinds of color-printing cannot end without mention of Masayoshi, or Keisai, who crossed cheerfully from one name to the other, style to style, school to school, retiring from daimyo service to become a lay monk. Like Hokusai, who admired him, Masayoshi transcends categories, and two of his books link themselves naturally with the later appearance, over many decades, of Hokusai's *Manga*. The first of these, *Jimbutsu Ryakuga-Shiki* ("Methods of Cursive Drawing of Figures"), 1799, belongs with such as we have seen in the work of Bumpo and Kanyosai, lively little sketches of people, plants, a few landscapes. The difference is in technique and printing, for these combine vigorous observation, and a characteristic color and graining, with such small use of outline in the flower-studies as makes them look like stencilling. On soft paper, this again pretends to be a manual for artists, extending to become its own work of art.

The companion to it, *Sansui Ryakuga-Shiki* ("Methods of Cursive Drawing of Landscapes"), appeared a year later [Plate 59]. This carried the same process further, with more color and larger sketches which change, as the pages turn, to double-page landscapes in their own style, with minimal outline or none, an incomparable book. Grey graining was essential to its effects, with pale orange and green. The conventions are Chinese, more honored in the breach than the observance. For graining of the grey one is grateful, as ever, to woodcutter and printer rather than to the artist.

Masayoshi was responsible also for a much-admired fish book, published in 1802, available with or without poems on pages of illustration; but this notion of poetry and picture appearing together leads conveniently to a slightly different subject.

*　　*　　*　　*　　*

THE interest and difference is that such works overlap with *surimono*. On that delightful subject Roger Keyes has written a large book, which he begins by explaining that the word means "a printed object" and could refer to text, a picture or both; but that it came to mean "two different types of privately distributed Japanese woodblock print: publications issued to announce or commemorate certain events like musical performances, and publications which combined a picture with verse." It is with the latter that we shall be concerned, and everything about it appeals within this subject: illustration and text together, as with many a book, small numbers and the notion of private printing.

The combination of picture with poem was natural to woodblock printing, where image and calligraphy formed one composition. It was not uncommon in French books, during the nineteenth century and after, for drawings or lithographs to wander across double pages; but compositors faced their problem of setting type to fit the empty spaces. The Japanese block-cutter prepared a single scheme of design without restraint of composing-stick, galley and furniture.

Though image and caption are always seen together, with *haiku* or other kinds of brief poems a special connection, spatial relationship, came easily. Masayoshi's fish book from 1802 was issued both ways, with poems or without, as often happened. Subject, color and the *finesse* of mica-dust make this a work of rare merit, yet one is conscious of space left for use. The asymmetry of Japanese books gave scope for variation.

A finer example of combined design, poem and picture is Taniguchi Gesso's *Haikai*

Hyaku Gasan ("One Hundred Haiku Poems Illustrated"), published at Kyoto and Wakayama in 1816, a black-and-grey work in two volumes which gives great pleasure whether or not one understands a word of the poems [Plate 60]. *Haiku* comes through poorly in translation, generally minor *aperçus* some distance from Western expectation. So we are free to appreciate print and design: the old fisherman with his birds and flares; a *Nanga* iris opposite the "northern" domestic elegance of a flute lesson; a sensuous tea-bowl; winter scene of hill and bamboo under snow; spring flowers, fruit, snow on a railing at the corner of one page below a suggestion of endless mist. These images needed the completion of large calligraphy, unity within one block; it is not surprising that names of the calligraphers for both volumes were given.

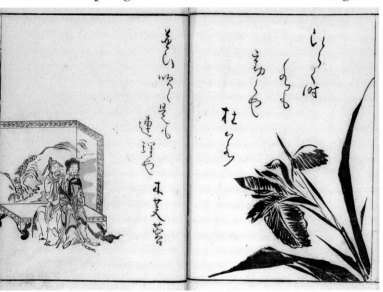

Plate 60. Taniguchi Gesso: from Haikai Hyaku Gasan, 1816

An earlier instance of the same concept is the work by Tachibana Minko, described as an artist "much too highbrow for the taste of his time, hence never famous," *Saiga Shokunin Burui* ("Book of Japanese Craftsmen"), two volumes issued in 1770 and again fourteen years later. This charming source-book of eighteenth-century Japanese men and women at work on their arts and crafts was color-printed, and each double-page illustration carries poetic text in running hand above, freely balancing the designs. Here is the gently colored second edition; coloring of the first was stronger, and has been much admired. Thus we see woodcut artists, painters, *Noh*-mask makers, weavers, brush makers, umbrella makers, prostitutes, musicians, potters; a social and artistic spectrum of people at work, sometimes as families or with apprentices, generally at home; a hard-laboring world but not without its flower vases, pot plants, and screens and blossom.

There is no doubt that *surimono* found its way into books, as a form of poetic illustration. An obscure example is here, using that art to elegant effect: *Ryuko Meibutsushi* ("Noted Products of Willow Street"), 1834, by a little-known painter, Sakuma Soan—or perhaps he wrote the book, engaging an anonymous illustrator. These pale-colored woodcuts, generally across two pages, spread curiously now and then to a third; the poems drop without symmetry, a facet of composition. On elegant paper and with no fading of red or mauve, this indeed suggests aesthetic life; comparable printing decorates the covers.

Surimono had its own life, to which some of the familiar artists contributed. By chance acquaintance it is simplest, as ever, to examine what is here; linked intriguingly to the Goncourts, inscribed "*A André Richard, en mémoire de Monsieur de Goncourt et en souvenir du Comte de Montesquieu,*" Proust's friend. *Surimono* rank as printed ephemera, often thrown away; it would not be easy now (though it was forty years ago, when Chester Beatty wanted them) to form a collection. Chester Beatty's four albums, together with a few separate prints, were catalogued by Roger Keyes and reproduced in those two large volumes mentioned above.

Ignorance of the language and inability to read the poems becomes frustrating, for one cannot identify the occasions they celebrate. To most Japanese people and Western scholars they remain—if that consoles us—incomprehensible. A *surimono* exhibited, at this moment of writing, in the Japan galleries of the British Museum has a caption explaining that the poem has not been deciphered. Words have many senses, we are told; the subject is subtle, calligraphy idiosyncratic.

This year's Christmas cards from Japan give some notion of *surimono*, but their methods are photographic, or computer-controlled, mass-productive, quite contrary to the real thing. *Surimono* could be Ukiyo-e in style, or not; it happens that my Goncourt-related albums and prints are mostly Shijo [Plates 61 & 62]. When poets and artists in that quarter of Kyoto met in groups or clubs, if the event were a success it was recorded afterwards in such private prints as these, prepared for members and a few friends. Often more than one artist shared a single design,

Plate 61. Large Shijo surimono

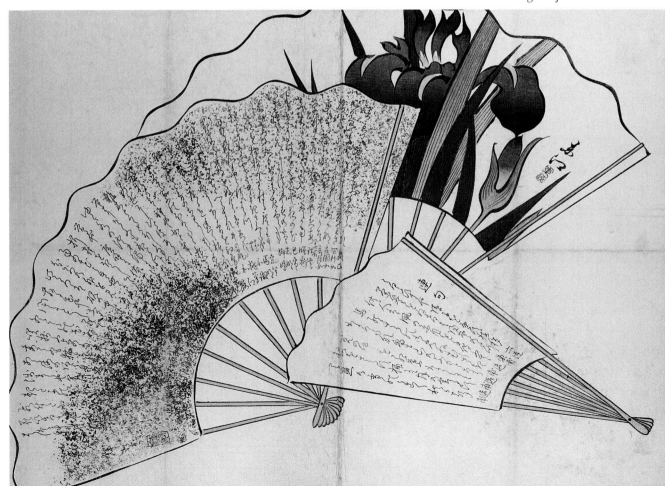

signed with their seals; then woodcut workshops were engaged, of course, to complete the job. Many brief poems, in delicate calligraphy, needed all the skills and received them; or there were only a few words to be cut, more prominently, balancing the drawing.

That was one kind of surimono—large, the designs bold and prominent or spare and reticent; often showing an ultimate *finesse* in woodblock color-printing: shades, textures, embossing, with special effects of gold, silver and mica; leaves and petals falling from white to pink, waterfalls printed by *gauffrage*, the unobtrusive use of many colors or none. A Swedish scholar, Louise Virgin, devotes her days to understanding and translating the poems from large Shijo surimono; her book is expected, and I can hardly wait. Many such prints survive in unique examples, much work cries out to be done.

Not all surimono were adorned with poems; the occasions ranged from concert programs to wedding announcements or any kind of information decorously presented—childbirth, moving house. Most were small, perhaps with text and no picture—the rarest indeed, for there was least temptation to preserve them. Those which survive are likely to be mounted in albums, a varied and delightful offering of surprises. No pleasure compares with leafing through albums, the key to their meaning an agreeable mystery.

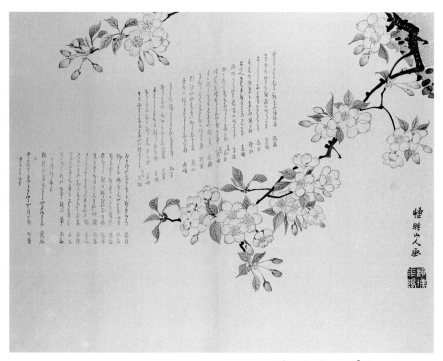

Plate 62. Large Shijo surimono

1. Outsize radishes, cultivated in Japan like leeks in Wales.

CHAPTER SEVEN
ILLUSTRATED BOOKS III

THE position of Ukiyo-e prints and books in the recent history of collecting (which means, I suppose, of values) is so bewildering that we have yet to wait for a critical balance. Arriving in Europe, we are told, as packing and stuffing, their merits were recognized by the Goncourt brothers in France. As this is supposed to be a book about collecting, an anecdote of values is not out of order. For twenty years I worked at Routledge and Kegan Paul, book publishers, who owned also the Kegan Paul Bookshop which occupied at that time a corner site opposite the British Museum. It was perhaps the best place in London for Japanese prints; everything excellent passed through that place. The mandate might now strike us as ludicrously large, "Oriental and African," as if that represented specialized knowledge across half the world. The point of my anecdote is a recollection from about 1960, when the publishing chairman remarked to his colleague in charge of sales, "You know, Carter, we shall have to give up buying Japanese prints, they're getting up to a hundred pounds." Such would now be twenty or thirty thousand pounds. The publishing company was sold and sold again. Its path to prosperity would have been to buy the finest Ukiyo-e prints, and cease publishing books. Yesterday I visited a friend who owns a decorative actor-print by Toyokuni, from those days, my wedding present. It would be beyond the horizons of generosity to think of choosing it for him now.

We may expect the graph of hyperbole to rise yet higher, for the willowy girls and multi-colored prints, before reaching its cruising height and descending—and the same may apply to Japanese verse. Both subjects combine in one of the conspicuously beautiful Ukiyo-e books, *Nishikizuri onna sanjurokkasen* ("Thirty-six Immortal Women Poets in Color Prints"), 1801, which has been translated and well reproduced in color. In a large, much-admired subject I confine this brief view to half a dozen well-known examples, and of them all the book of women poets strikes me as incomparable.

As color-printing from 1801 it represents the climax of an art: shading, multiple impressions for perhaps a dozen colors from different blocks, patterning of kimonos, the hair of these elegant girls which travels like waterfalls down their complex silks. The unfaded mauves and reds could only survive thus in a closed book. Opposite each imagined portrait is one of her poems, upon cloud shapes in four and five colors across the pages; and their calligraphy—the point of departure for this book—was by the girl pupils of an Edo writing-master, Hanagata Yoshiakira. One of them, Toyota Mine, was six years old. Beyond each outside margin in running-hand the child's name and address were given. "Although we are now more struck by its colorful illustrations," Andrew Pekarik writes in his introduction to the excellent paperback published by Tuttle, "the album originally functioned as a publicity vehicle to show off the accomplishments of the young girls whose calligraphy records the poems."

Low comment upon certain forms of Japanese art flows easily, as does a pretense of appreciation. Reading these old, brief, formal "poems" in translation, with explanatory paragraphs, one dares question the common sense of such generous treatment of commonplace sentiments. Here is, at random, one of the immortal poems:

> Men, without thinking
> That they are in fact lies,
> Have made promises,
> What hurts is this life of mine
> Where change is habitual.

And another:

> Everywhere I look
> Cherry trees are starting to bloom.
> Right up to the base
> Of lovely Mount Yoshino
> Whose blossoms are deep within.

The translator comments: "What started as another harmless poem on pretty cherry blossoms somehow manages in its short span to generate successive waves

Plate 63. Hokusai: frontispiece to the "Thirty-six Immortal Women Poets," 1801

of suggestive meaning that reach into the deepest levels (*oku*) of experience." With all reverence for puns and allusive ambiguities, this seems to stretch the courtesies to breaking point.

There is a frontispiece to this book of the poets and their poems, across two pages, by Hokusai: a courtly group has crossed a footbridge, deep in talk, followed by servants bearing baggage and an infant, while three children resting on the slope above, with bill-hook and basket, point down laughing at the fashionable world [Plate 63]. Green cloud-forms at the top link this with similar designs which accompany the poems—a sensitive touch from the block-cutters perhaps. Hokusai's all-male conversation piece serves as comment or chorus to the action, sets a tone against excessive sentiment.

Hosoda Eishi was the artist, commissioned by Hanagata Yoshiakira to draw these thirty-six women with their poetic clothes and hair [Plate 64]; names of the block-cutters are given. This trio came last, not first, in the planning: "Finally," he wrote, "I direct the woodblock carvers and artist to set to work."

Boundaries for schools of art are as confusing as definitions of a private press. I find within the limits of Ukiyo-e formality, manners, a graceful style of life—

Plate 64. Eishi: from the "Thirty-six Immortal Women Poets," 1801

contrasted with an artist's more private visions and impressions in Shijo, Nanga, Rimpa, "and other Related Schools," to borrow from the title of Mitchell's bibliography. Theater, samurai life and legend come within orbit for Ukiyo-e; wit and satire, if present, keep their distance.

Hillier's *magnum opus* paid more than adequate attention to *shunga*, the erotic prints and books from which earlier English historians had turned away; an intriguing subject, if only because they may puzzle us by total absence (for this viewer) of sexual excitement. Gross and explicit they are, but I think those who seek pornography will find them disappointing. If the Japanese feel untroubled by guilt in sex, as one is often told, their art reflects this in a detached freedom of observation, making genitals and the antics of love neither more nor less observable, worth recording, than other facets of daily or nightly lives.

Though legend and theater from Japan are obscure to most of us—compared with, say, blossom, insects and fashion—they have a high place in Ukiyo-e. None is more admired than Sharaku's actor-prints with their liberal mica-ground, even when creased and soiled. Beside me is a humble book in samurai tradition, Kuniyoshi's *Ichiyu Gafu*, 1830, Ichiyu being an early name of this artist whose pseudonyms, like his works, were prolific. The limited coloring in grey and pink, the might of elements and man, descend from very early painted war-scrolls—and connect with modern strip cartoon.

Easier to accept, and infinitely finer, is Utamaro's "Picture-book of Selected Insects" (*Ehon Mushi-erabi*), 1788 [Plate 65], which flies straight to the highest branch; yet one may question why this always belongs among the best-known Ukiyo-e books, Kitagawa Utamaro being an artist of that school. No "school" confines such designs—but that subject becomes wearisome.

Utamaro's insect book shocks with color and invention each time it is opened. A childish pleasure in seeming always to discover among the fruit and foliage another insect,

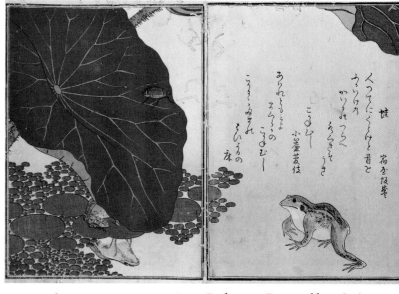

Plate 65. From Utamaro's Insect Book, 1788: Frogs and lotus leaf

takes one inside the plant to the abundant life exploring it. In this poetic triumph of color-printing and delicacy of spirit, insects are shown with such sympathy that one cannot imagine the gross act of squashing them. I notice now, in what had only been plant-design before, a beetle's back descending the far side of a leaf, as a grey worm weaves among the stems. My favorite device is a frog, alone to the right, watching another frog on a lotus leaf; but a larger leaf hides it, so we see only a reflection of the frog observed. Such conceits are both literary and linear.

If the heart of Ukiyo-e rests among geisha, the slender girls groomed for men's pleasure—looking so bored and distant in *shunga* prints—this part of Japanese art is not for feminists. Utamaro, specializing in the subject, produced his *Seiro Ehon Nenju-gyoji* ("Picture Book of the Green Houses: Events throughout the Year") in 1804, but these were not the greenhouses of a Surrey suburb [Plate 66]. Elegant it was, blameless prelude and aftermath, men traditionally gazing from the balcony as through screens one sees a servant speeding with tea, or *sake*, on her tray.

Plate 66. From Utamaro's "Picture Book of the Green Houses," 1804

Here is nothing gross as visitors smoke and converse, the women tend them and cook, snow falls; passers-by eavesdrop, the girls point and, then as now, shield their faces to smile. This essay in the manner of restraint—processional, observant, a document of normality, nothing more riotous than blind-man's buff—crossing two centuries in two unfaded volumes, with small incident less noticeable than color-patterned gowns, ends with a double-page of the artist himself probably at work upon his mighty screen-painting of an eagle, its multi-colored plumage reflecting patterned kimonos of several girls who watch from beyond the tatami.

Two works from the late eighteenth century (1770 and 1776) occupy a peak of calm, elegance and printing in this most characteristic Ukiyo-e subject, the geisha, or girls of the Yoshiwara district, or Green Houses: Harunobu's *Ehon Seiro Bijin Awase* ("Picture Book Comparing the Beauties of the Green Houses"), 1770, and the combined work of two artists, Kitao Shigemasa and Katsukawa Shunsho, *Seiro Bijin Awase Sugata Kagami* ("Rival Beauties of the Green Houses"), 1776. Harunobu was a pioneer of such work in color-printed books; the other two produced three volumes of more varied design, from that world of women. Each is from a society totally disappeared, mercifully beyond recall, and of an incomparable mannered excellence. Hillier calls the 1776 volumes "the first masterpiece in book form to be published by Tsutaya Jusaburo" and quotes a translated paragraph from the preface by Jusaburo, who wrote:

> Here in these three volumes of Snow, Moon, and Flowers, which I have entitled *A Mirror of Rival Beauties*, the two flourishing artists of the day—Kitao and Katsukawa—labouring with brush and palette, have with indefatigable zeal depicted the graceful forms of the courtesans of the Enclosure as they appear when on promenade or within the precincts of their elegant chambers.

It is not clear whether the "rival beauties" are of snow, moon and flowers, or between the girls themselves; everything in the book would suggest the former, for only apathy and decorum occupy the latter.

We are so accustomed to a convention of season-by-season, or night and day, that the trinity of snow, moon and flowers arrives with surprising charm. The first volume has a frontispiece of violets and marigolds, and pauses halfway for a double-page of irises; the second of peonies and morning glory with a halfway break for chrysanthemums; the third, with fewer prints and a text, shows in bold angles the entrance doors in winter, a barrel, wooden wash-tubs stacked above it, a dark conifer.

Within each we see the girls at their calligraphy, smoking long pipes, watching a caged bird, playing cat's cradle, plucking strings of the *samisen*, picking blossom, talking, painting. They watch passing birds, passing seasons. Most beautiful are winter prints, where they contemplate a large flower-arrangement against the screen-painting of Fuji in snow. If it was an idle world, they deserved their quiet after always dressing perfectly, no hint of disarray; and the snow scenes make clear it was, in winter, an exceedingly cold world; no concessions to the season beyond an outer garment wrapped up to the neck. Slippers sink into snow, a hand points to the branch as if snow were blossom. They play cards, arrange themselves by the bowl of ash with several small logs smoldering; we come with relief to spring. One double page of winter shows two girls watching as a third pulls up her wooden ladle from the pool in a rock's hollow—lifting with it the whole surface of ice in which it had frozen.

Unlike Utamaro's books three decades later, this was the publisher's ideal world of elegance—never a man in sight or, it seems, thought.

It makes no sense to turn from the nineteenth-century illustrated books without viewing one or another of the Hokusai albums; and the example I choose with reason is his "Hundred Views of Fuji" (*Fugaku Hyakkei*) published in three volumes, the first two appearing in 1834-5 and the third, perhaps wrongly regarded as inferior, from a different publisher after an interval of fifteen years. As Hokusai was the most perverse of artists, trespassing across all boundaries and confined by

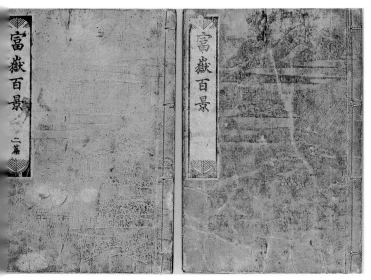

no school, this masterpiece in black-and-grey may be considered among books of prints strongly colored. Here is Edmond de Goncourt's copy of the first issue, the two volumes from the 1830s in their embossed pink covers [Plate 67] with the "falcon's feather" title labels, and his inscription:

Edition à la plume de faucon, édition de la plus grande rareté, et, dont on ne connait que deux volumes publiés sur les trois qu'ont les editions suivandes.

So he settled for the two in pink covers, but many or most of the prints in Volume Three seem to me of equal merit, and that orange volume now lives with the other two.

I am brought back to my schoolmaster's comment, "You can't *describe* a *picture*." As to the printing, comparison with a good (though not a first) edition of Hokusai's *Manga* or Sketchbooks, their fifteen volumes stretching from 1814 to 1878, declares the extraordinary quality of these first-issue views of Fuji. If it were necessary to open the first volume for exhibition, I might choose a double-page showing the snow-white mountain behind palest grey suggestions of tree-shapes in mist, expressed by slight embossing and two impressions for the greys, from different blocks; while baskets and tools are carried up steep rock, clear but half-snowy, near us to the right [Plate 68].

Plate 68. From Hokusai's "Hundred Views." Myth and mist below Fuji

Hillier, who calls this "the crown upon Hokusai's work," has described the artist's wish "to make a set of landscape variations on the theme of Fuji, interweaving its form with the lives of people of all types, causing it to dominate the landscape or to be half-hidden or barely discernible through or behind the foreground elements—bathed in sunshine, or suddenly illuminated by lightning, or veiled by driving rain." The notion of "Views" of Fuji tells little, for this most inventive work records all life under its shadow. Sometimes one seeks the mountain's image as if the picture were a puzzle—and there it is, reflected upside down in a cup of *sake*, amazing the drinker

Plate 69. From Hokusai's "Hundred Views"

[Plate 69]; in rough and calm water, or a mirror; through a bamboo plant, fishermen's net or spider's web; viewed for itself through springtime blossom; through a screen, or in small black geometry as a triangle resting upon the tall rectangle of a boat's sail. This unity of people, landscape, myth and the seasons, reduced now to tour-buses and the hotel window, brings back the concept of Fuji as a god.

Japanese illustrated books, or albums of illustrations, do not end with the Meiji period or with woodcut, but the absorption or adaptation of foreign influences is a difficult subject to judge. French and German art crossed to Japan, with no more effort than junk food and baseball; *japonisme* arrived in Europe. Yet the examples, when one sees them, are irresistible. Four volumes of design, like a pattern book, by Furutani Korin in a Japanese art-deco manner from 1905–06, possibly using silk-screen together with woodcut, are wonderfully inventive in the adaptation of old subjects—blossom, waves, snow-on-trees, Fuji, plant forms, landscape—to a recent idiom, in brilliant color. This is Rimpa updated; such albums no doubt inspired a whole spectrum of dress-design or kimono fabric, West and East. The final volume was devoted, predictably, to variations upon the theme of bamboo [Plate 70].

Plate 70. Furutani Korin: from album of bamboo designs, 1905

Kamisaka Sekka may be taken to represent an adventurous trend in the earlier twentieth century, living from 1866 to 1942 and rejoicing in those wicked chemical dyes which I was taught years ago, at Kegan Paul, to avoid as in bad taste. They had been commonly used since the middle of the nineteenth century; I am reminded of that tempting album of *bejin* by Toyokuni III, which so foolishly remained in Tokyo. Sekka brought Rimpa freedom daringly into modern art, using solid color with fearless strength; yet the old skills of gradation and shading came when called, as in a double-page of morning glory climbing up poles of bamboo. The strength

Plate 71. From Kamisaka Sekka, Momoyogusa, *1909*

of his designs in three large volumes called *Momoyogusa* ("World of Things"), 1909, is some distance beyond description; there had been nothing like this before, nor would there be again, for he represents the end of a tradition. Audrey Yoshiko Seo of the Virginia Commonwealth University at Richmond, writing on Sekka in the December 1993 issue of *Orientations*, refers to

> . . . the three-volume illustrated book *Momoyogusa* ("World of Things") that firmly established the artist within the ranks of the greatest Japanese designers. In these stunning illustrations, Sekka's genius in modern design shines through, combining elements of humor, whimsy and charm with the elegance traditionally associated with Japanese decorative arts. The images possess a radiant clarity of composition and design that sets Sekka apart, revealing his vision as an artist of the twentieth century. In keeping with his appreciation of traditional Rimpa aesthetics, Sekka often used familiar Rimpa subjects such as irises, plum blossoms and the thirty-six immortal poets.

Among many surprises of composition and vision I choose two powerful examples with roots in old Japan: the black-robed priest, bare-legged, face hidden as if the wind were blowing from our direction, walking through water or tall grass, holding his hat against snow [Plate 71]; and a boy flute-player resting against the black back of an ox so vast that it spills beyond the pages, emblem for that most sympathetic Zen myth of seeking, then controlling, one's true self [Plate 72].

Plate 72. From Kamisaka Sekka, Momoyogusa, *1909*

CHAPTER EIGHT
SOME PHRASE-BOOKS
FROM OLD JAPAN

T HE visual elegance of old books from Japan, printed and manuscript, scroll or codex, explains the uncomprehending desire of a Westerner to collect them. Courtly stories illustrated with a brilliant miniature detail recalling Persian eighteenth-century art need no apologia; more surprising, from earliest days to the Meiji period and after, is the excellence of workaday stuff—pots, sacks, documents, dictionaries. From the seventh century when that great imperial collection, kept now at the Shoso-in, was formed, such material was preserved and cherished and survives.

Japanese phrase-books should be viewed against that background. As Japan remained isolated for many centuries, a need for them arose only in the second half of the nineteenth century when the Emperor Meiji encouraged contact with the West. The earliest of five examples in front of me is from 1855, a few years before the Meiji era, but wider trade links were already developing. If we associate phrase-books with tourist travel, smiling at advice to send for the British Consul in times of trouble and annoyance, our response to these from Japan should be different because they were made for the business of trade; and Japanese publishers devised them, in their own way. The invariable form was to have three lines of languages: Japanese, English, and the English transliterated as a guide to correct pronunciation.

From the eighth century to the nineteenth, not much changed in the methods of Eastern printing. Movable type, though initiated in Korea and practiced in Japan, suited our brief alphabet but not the Chinese syllabary; thus block-books, begun and abandoned in fifteenth-century Europe, prevailed in the East for more than a thousand years. These phrase-books from the second half of the nineteenth century were cut in wood, page by page. For a few years in the early Meiji period copper was used instead of wood, as will be explained. Lithography, appropriate for Eastern texts and illustration, arrived there surprisingly late. The policy of isolation had its disadvantages.

So the phrase-books, charmingly produced, were more closely in touch than other forms of literature with a real world of their moment. They were used, but the old paper covers with their title slips survive: yellow, chocolate-color, purple, decorative as ever. Japanese books were never bound in hard covers, but remain as anyone might have seen them in the bookshops of that time. Such English catalogue description as "uncut in original wrappers" is irrelevant.

In the several examples one must first admire the skills of woodcut artists, the makers of block books, shaping unfamiliar words from an alphabet they had not learned to use. Most art being more imitative than creative, they earn their place in the story; following written copy in clerkly style, or falling into a particular habit of Western script which came most naturally and still does—for we recognize it today on notice boards throughout Japan.

These skilled workers made occasional mistakes of several kinds. They might misunderstand the pronunciation of an instructor, or use wrong spelling. Faults in grammar came from authors or editors who, then as now, thought they knew another language well enough; and if a phrase sounds curiously old-fashioned they were perhaps using some Dutch-English phrase-book from an earlier period, when the Dutch had special trading privileges at Nagasaki. How else can one explain, for example, in a book from 1873, the delightful request: "There is the periwig-maker be so kind as to cut my hair"?

Some doubt lingers as to whether these were made for visitors or locals; Japanese books open backwards (as we see them) like Hebrew books, but here either method may be found. For systematic reference a knowledge of Japanese was needed; those who lacked it faced a confusing succession of words, such as *sour, sweet, bitter, picture, chamber-pot.* The tendency was to graduate from alphabets through vocabulary to phrases and dialogue.

In the first and fattest of this group, *Kaei Tsugo* ("Beautiful English Communication") made in 1855, the block-cutter had as his model a scribe who enjoyed elaborate curly capitals. Though fine lines and a running hand suggest lithography, it was all cut in wood. After one page of undistinguished alphabet we move to vocabulary, in which some very un-Japanese food evokes a high standard of life:

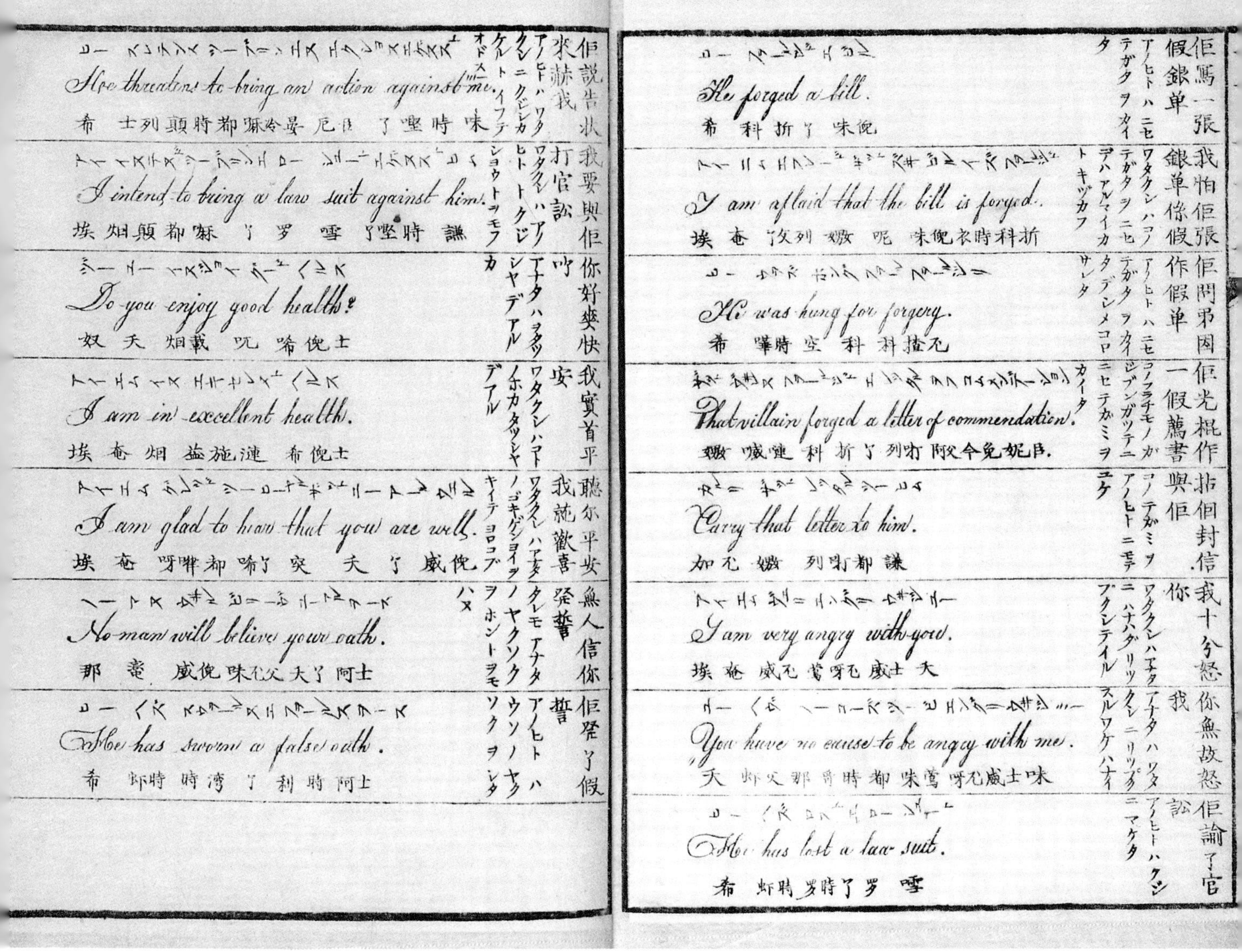

He threatens to bring an action against me.

I intend to bring a law suit against him.

Do you enjoy good health?

I am in excellent health.

I am glad to hear that you are well.

No man will believe your oath.

He has sworn a false oath.

He forged a bill.

I am afraid that the bill is forged.

He was hung for forgery.

That villain forged a letter of commendation.

Carry that letter to him.

I am very angry with you.

You have no cause to be angry with me.

He has lost a law suit.

Plate 73. Kaei Tsugo, 1855: "He forged a bill. . ."

Baked oyster pie, Stock-fish, Beef suet, Carambola tart, Toast, Veal, Beef's tongue, Dried venison appear in one column, as if copied from a ship's menu. *Toast* stamps it as British.

Phrases and dialogue provide social history. A whole short-story combines with one familiar error in this succession [Plate 73]:

> He forged a bill.
> I am aflaid that the bill is forged.
> He was hung for forgery.

recalling the Reverend William Dodd and his tragic fate a century earlier.

"Tell the cooly to bring some coal" is unlikely to be heard now, but the insincerity of "Give much or little it makes no difference" remains unchanged. Such melodramatic phrasing as "poisonous hearted," "draw near," "Bid him pass on before," will not now be heard in trading circles. Wrong grammar ("I understand it very few") is rare, and minor spelling mistakes ("His trail taks place today") are easily understandable. "The lack of the head," "official tittles," "unbreached cloth" were small aberrations. The whole book formed a fine achievement.

CHAPTER EIGHT: SOME PHRASE-BOOKS FROM OLD JAPAN

Three of the five date from 1873, a vintage year. One small volume with yellow covers, *Eikaiwa Soyaku* ("English Conversation Translation") launches into useful phrases without the preparation of alphabet or syllable, advancing fast from school to adult life. Perhaps the severity of education made that possible—this is how it starts:

"I am going to school ti strikes nine o clock."
"make haste it is mach later."
"that is not possible."
"you come very late prayers have been said already."
"I have been detained by my uncle sir."
"you deceive me I fear. you are not half dressed.
        that sluttishness displeases me. you have not
        washed your hands and face. you got up too late I believe."
"forgive me sir I shall be more careful in the future."

This is an interesting book in several ways. The writing has an un-Japanese slope, and *sluttishness* seems a foreign term; yet every word was copied by a Japanese worker upon wood, nothing transferred, for no European teacher could have written *ti* for *it*.

School passes and he is ordering a suit from the Tailor, in the English style ("I hav followed long enough the french fashion"):

"must the waist be so long?"
"without doubt and the skirts short."
"how is it with the collar?"
"it must be high and very broad."
"you will make me a singular dress."
"when shall I have my suit?"
"the next week."
"I hope you are a man of your word."
"I will stand to my promise."
"it is a tailors promise."
"you like to jest sir."

Clothes, prices and bad temper are the author's concerns, all explained in a pleasant running hand. There is trouble about the purchase of proper cloth:

"I cant sell it under five shillings."
"oh! you joke I believe. you ask out of the way.
        will you bate nothing of it."
"I make but one word. it is indeed very cheap."
"it stands me in more than you bid me for it. I cunt
        do it without losing by it."
"you are pleased to say so. I mast give you what you
        ask then. there is your money."

And that was followed by every sort of complaint ("see how ugly that looke. as to the trousers they are too wide. they are wretchedly made. the trousers mast be rectified.")

Who wrote it, one wonders? A bad tailor whose clever memory allowed him to recall phrases heard in his shop? These were not the words of any foreign school-master. An altercation at the cobbler comes next:

> "where is my shoeinghorn? stamp your foot upon the
> ground. there your foot is in. there is not the
> least wrinkle in them. they fit you to a hair."
> "they pinch me too much. they are too narrow. and
> the toes are too sharp."

After the lost shoehorn and vigorous stamping our sympathy is with the customer, who ends wearily:

> "I will have shoes which are neither too narrow nor
> too wide."
> "you are very hard to please sir."

Again the question arises, whether all this was for Japanese patrons of an English shop or foreign visitors to a local shop. Made-to-measure shoes were not in the Japanese tradition.

Aggression leads Mr. N to higher life from which he could look back to the wretched days at school.

> "he is an illdesigning person. mr. N grew angry and
> has hambled him very much. at last the coxcomb made
> himself ridiculous. and every one laughed at him."

English is the secret of advancement. "it is at present the universal language." The sequence has a wonderful ending:

> "it is not for the sake of interest he marries her.
> he will be happy with such an accomplished person.
> they are happy on both sides."

Variety provides unexpected pleasure in handling these several books; they were not made to formula, one publisher imitating another. Visually and verbally each was his own man. The chocolate volume from 1873, *Eigaku Kyoju* ("English Learning Textbook"), has a botchy mathematical layout which seems to offer business and system, comprehension, success; for local consumption this wears provincial dress; no foreigner shaped the script or devised such method. English words appear vertically down Japanese columns of grammar; there is an observant focus upon forms of lettering, and an effort to sort out pronunciation. Much of the text, in Japanese style, crosses both sides of a double page. It is my favorite of the five, an everyday tool for some small shop. "I will buy 1000 tubs toukiyau oil. The tubs contains 30 sho, Fish oil is not mixed with it." "To walk in, Here is the femele hanu writin."

Though the code of dots and accents defeats me, it was remarkable to have heard seven ways to pronounce the letter A, as in fame, fat, air, father, last, all, and what. The different alphabets interest me even more, from heavy caps and lower case as found in printed books, to handwriting and such ornamental letters as might be used in embroidery. The "Italic Small Lotters" [Plate 74] are undistinguished, the embroidered capitals have no name. Though this will never come under scrutiny from bibliographers, more than one hand can be detected in its making. "Preposition," "Conjunction," "Interjection" are perfect though vertical and in fine lines; other terms were less evenly cut, with erratic spelling ("A high prrich," "Whele wus that linen printed"). Cutter A manages "Som ms." Cutter B fills the gap (almost) with "et" but a little above the line like a correc-

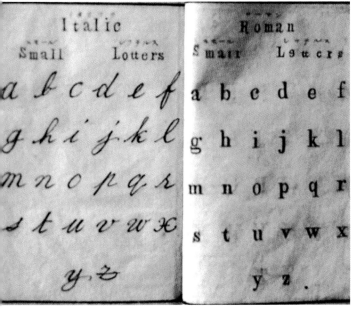

Plate 74. Eigaku Kyoju, 1873: "Italic Small Lotters"

tion. Again we have the forged bill, this time he was hung "for forgry," and the adage "If good I will buy, if bab i wont."

The purple book, same date, opens in European style and its covers are faintly embossed with a chicken-wire pattern. All five volumes used an arrangement of boxes and borders; most were printed on such paper as we now envy, with never a trace of foxing, offset or fading. If any notion of superiority hides behind this report of phrase and spelling, the thought of paper used for comparable productions in Europe at that time should banish it.

This work has an English title page cut in running hand, as are all its English words and phrases. The title reads: *"Phrases in English and Japanese, Elementary for the children. (Matsuoka Saikiyo). First edition. Anno 5 Mei Zi."* Its Japanese title is *Waei Tsugo* ("Japanese-English Communication"). The date brings to mind French books issued in years after the Revolution. Japanese people have an elegant habit of pressing leaves of the ginko tree and placing them between pages of their favorite books. Several are in this volume, perhaps suggesting family use at home, though it advances quickly from vocabulary and numbers to commerce. I admire a message which should echo in the brains of all book-collectors: "If the article is only good never mind the price buy it and bring it here," followed by cheerful news "I am buying them all at once."

As often, the level of accuracy varies from scrupulous copying to a rough guess. Thus after the almost correct "Difficlt to carry on a large business with a small capital," and complex clinical terms carefully transcribed, we come upon "Oacea Pssae Tshe" for which I suppose no model was found and nothing would do but a brave plunge. "I sell them for zeady many" is dubious, "Opium does not sell very wellenow" was marked with a ginko leaf. Real misunderstanding could have caused the constant error of "Father in low," "Son in low," "Mother in low," "Sister in low," for relatives are not so honorably regarded by Westerners as in Japan.

My final example is different, smaller in format, about fourteen years later, upon— I suspect—machine-made paper. Everything is delightful still, but the world has visibly changed. Issued in Osaka by an enterprising publisher, Aoki Suzando, the title on faded green covers is *Convenient Book for English*; Japanese title, *Eigo Jizai* ("Fluent English"). Aoki was something of a publicist. Among several examples for corresponding in English, near the end of this volume we find:

> Dear Sir,
>> During my last visit at your house, you were pleased to call my attention to a book entitled "Illustrated guide book for travellers round the world" which I remember to have been a work of so much interest, that I feel inclined to peruse it. . .

I have them beside me now, the seven attractive volumes, a series well known in Japan, a local answer to Baedecker—published, as will be no surprise, in Osaka by Aoki Suzando. Another group of seven informed the Japanese about their own land. They will be viewed in the next chapter.

Aoki turns up elsewhere in the *Convenient Book for English*, notably at his own bookshop under the heading WITH A BOOK SELLER where this exchange is printed:

> Are you Aoki Suzando? You have received lately an
>> assortment of English books, I should like to see them.
>
> You are very welcome sir. They were not unpacked
>> before this morning. You shall have the first sight of them.
>
> Are they all new books?
>
> Not all, sir. Some are new, some are old publications. Have
>> you found any thing that suits you?
>
> Yes; here is a note of the books I wish to have.
>
> Is there any thing more you would like?
>
> I want some conversation book.
>
> Whose conversation book do you wish for?
>
> I wish for the new conversation book which is just published.
>
> The price is only twenty-five yen but its value
>> can't be estimated with money.

It will be in much demand surely.

May I offer you any thing else?

I should wish to have Wedas ichimamben.

Have you Johnson's dictionary?

What do you ask for it?

One must admire the internal advertisement, its nearness to Johnson's Dictionary, two great neighbors in the same department.

In transcribing from Aoki's book I have slightly modernized the spelling as a matter of course, for this is a modern book; old spelling belongs to a different world, an aspect of its charm, though always in doubtful taste. Modernized Chaucer is deplorable, minor changes in Boswell or Chesterfield would not be improper. The phrases in Aoki are not always flawless: "We hop shall have a rain." "There is no wind blow."

But the great change was in pictorial definition. All his vocabulary is explained in fine-line vignettes of curious detail, twelve to each page, about six hundred and fifty of them. *Harp* ("*Haip*") is represented by a *koto*, *Bank* by an indeterminate pastoral scene—nothing to do with money—and *Bottle* shows a kettle, *Privy* is incomprehensible; but in their scope the pictures are accurate and clever. Of equal interest is the technique, for it seems that this whole book was produced from metal plates, printed intaglio. As no plate marks are detectable, they would have existed outside the page area. The very fine lines (not always clearly printed) of these vignettes could not have been managed in wood. Etching was a possibility, but no relief process is imaginable. Aoki was an innovator. This and all the guide books have marbled edges, and are collected for that curious reason, the earliest use in Japan of Western marbling techniques.

They enjoyed preparing their books, writing imaginary letters to each other. Mr. Hushio was no doubt on the staff.

Osaka, October 2th 1886

Dear T. Aoki.

As today is very fine weather, we will take a walk in the Garden of Sumyoshi after breakfast and afterward to and take tea at some restaurant where we will amuse ourselves till the evening, do not forget to come as soon as you have dined.

Yours truly,

T. Hushio.

We have an illustration of the envelope and how to seal it, with his address:

Dear T. Aoki

Andojimachi 4 chiome

Osaka

It sounds very civilized; one would like to have been there.

CHAPTER NINE
MEISHO-ZUE

I<small>NTENDING</small> to follow a light-hearted essay on early Meiji-period phrase books with a second part on comparable guide books, I looked again at earlier, purely Japanese, examples of this genre; but they are to be approached in a different spirit.

The phrase was *meisho-zue*, which means "guide to famous places." Examples exist from the seventeenth century, but as travel even within Japan was then discouraged there would have been small demand for them. Better-known examples are from the late eighteenth century and early nineteenth—and the idea continued, in varying form, to our own time. I thought of taking several of these longish works which are here, the results of book-browsing in Tokyo over the years, and writing about them as brief prelude to an essay on the entertaining Baedecker-type guide books of the last quarter of the nineteenth century; but as so often, those earlier books threaten to take control and need to be viewed more carefully.

Jack Hillier has a good short chapter on the *meisho-ki*, as they seem to be called generically, but he writes with the slant of an art historian and *meisho-zue* belong equally across the border in social history. Chibbett pointed out that the street-scenes of ordinary life in such books had their influence upon the development of Ukiyo-e art.

Ukiyo-e and Shijo both have their place in the *meisho-zue*. For "floating world" substitute "passing moment," and the two concepts join. Ukiyo-e has overtones of elegance, as with Utamaro's tall draped girls, but not always; Shijo suggests common life, fun, street nuisance, busy shops, small perceptions—but not always; they overlap.

The guide-books to famous places provide problems in description, for they are long—but full of illustration, and difficult to skip. The Tokyo *meisho-zue* of 1834–36 by Hasegawa Settan, a well-known example, runs to twenty volumes, so one must be limited to showing very few from among them, thus destroying the experience; for their charm is in travelling through the whole journey. But they are black-and-white, which is easy to reproduce; something may be conveyed, from a form of Japanese book which seems at present rather little known, and not much collected—and for that rare surprise one becomes truly grateful.

Plate 75. Miyako Meisho Zue: *Shrine, Kyoto*

One delightful work is among the better known: *Miyako Meisho Zue* or "Famous Places of the Eastern Capital" [Kyoto], by Takehara Shunchosai, eleven volumes published in 1780 [Plates 75–85]. Color-printing was approaching a fine period then, but these are in the long tradition of black-and-white line, with occasional dark-inked areas, of which there must then have been many master craftsmen. As always in Japanese books, artist and wood-cutter cooperated, one interpreting the other, but they were not the same; the artist-print was a much later development in Japan. The perfect sympathy by which those anonymous wood-cutters and the printers of their blocks adapted the spontaneous quality of the artists is constantly astonishing.

As these volumes of *Miyako Meisho Zue* were illustrated in this unchanging technique, so also they reflect unchanged life; for Japan in 1780 had preserved its isolation through almost two centuries of Tokugawa rule. A degree of calm had settled, without threat of revolution. Going through it I noted that this is "a classless book," absolute in the assumptions of class differences: an impression from the presence of them all, none deserving the artist's attention less than another. Within a general prevalence of hills, woods, roofs, streets, the panorama of temple roofs and precincts, are common events, ceremony, people of any rank passing and greeting or grimacing their thoughts on the highway. Chibbett's comment about their influence upon Ukiyo-e art is understood in this context.

As to art or life or social history, the distinctions are difficult. German woodcuts of the fifteenth century were generally reckoned to be crude and of small artistic merit, until William Morris pointed to their expressive strength. Morris, who knew nothing of Japanese street-life, might well have enjoyed these simple reports.

The character of paper and line governed such productions. Though popular, they were for the educated and literate, for there is plenty of text between hundreds of illustrations. The bed on which all this rests (to use a restaurant metaphor) is a long series of calm panoramas in the Chinese manner, of sloping roofs and temple gardens, more and less distant; it would be wrong to ignore those beautiful double-page impressions of eighteenth-century Kyoto, to focus only upon common life in the streets. This elegant scene struck visitors three centuries ago; each temple and shrine is labelled, as was appropriate in a guide book. Trees and blossom received conventional treatment in Chinese style, clouds and mist as in the old *Yamato-e*; people in such context recall stick-pictures, or insects. Woodcutting, printing, composition are unerring as one would expect. Of the total number of full-page or double-page woodcuts in these eleven volumes, most are mountain and temple panoramas of this sort [Plate 75].

All the occasional episodes and moments, captured as in a camera from routine days, are spaced among the permanence of hill and temple. In such a spectrum of

Plate 76. Miyako Meisho Zue: *Making sake from rice*

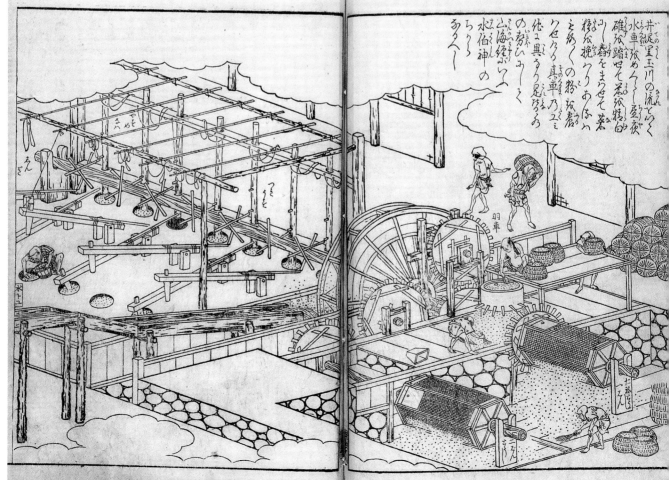

activities the artist's choice was random. Craftsmen were also shopkeepers in years before middlemen intervened to take their profit; so we see whole families of fan-makers, cloth-dyers, thatch-makers, potters, vegetable-growers, *sake*-makers, weavers. Such were the ordinary affairs of Kyoto or anywhere else, scenes of family life, social truth [Plate 76].

Plate 77. Miyako Meisho Zue: *Making and selling fans*

The thatcher, almost naked, on a rainy day smokes his pipe, waves his mallet at well-dressed passers-by who brave the storm. Dry under shelter, he squats by a smooth rock as working surface; behind, his wife watches and carries the bald-headed baby at her back. The domesticity of cooking-pots contrasts with a prospect of a wet walk over the mountain.

The potter, clothed with more dignity, works at his wheel on the raised platform of his shop, not distracted by chatter from a family in the street outside: three

CHAPTER NINE: MEISHO-ZUE

children, an infant pleading to be lifted up; their father, a large fish in his basket, pausing on the bench to scratch his foot. The potter's shaping tools like thorns are on a shelf, two stools of finished tea-bowls beside him and varied sample shelves of his work above.

The fan-makers provide a cheerful scene: humble folk hoist baskets of fish in the street outside, a well-dressed couple enjoy their toy dolls; a samurai departs with the fan he has chosen, two graceful girls offer others for sale, a third kneels on the platform showing examples to a customer—and at the back, behind open screens, the maker is at work [Plate 77]. These are circular painted fans with handles, for breeze on a hot day, not folding fans. "Guide to Famous Places in the Eastern Capital"? The diversions of a shop and life passing, as anywhere.

There was less time for fun at the weaving loom, which spreads its network of production with some text across two pages: two looms, serious work at the shuttle, formal dress, the woman of the house responsible above for setting a pattern. Posts and crossbeams of the looms are shaped like approaches to a shrine.

From these specific activities anyone might pause in a restaurant, or tea room. Such passivities were and are the essence of peace, there or anywhere else. In Japan one still finds, indoors and outside the restaurant, platforms rather than tables, where friends sit together. Platforms are places for relaxation, whether eating or resting, contemplating, viewing blossom or a sunset. Restaurants are often found outside temples, where a hot climb suggests pause for refreshment. To the far right of a double page (Vol. III) is the start of a high temple arch; nearby they prepare food on small sticks like a barbecue—sections of fish, which are chopped at a low bench. A samurai family watches and waits, feeds or teases the begging dog; people enter and leave the gate of the shrine; it is summer, with leaves on the trees.

In a particularly merry restaurant scene (Vol. VII) one customer who has taken too much *sake* raises his bowl to the attractive girl who brought it and grips her wrist as she draws away. Several who pass in the road turn back to watch, amused. Blocks of fish wait in a tub to be chopped, another girl walks with a tray, dish, chopsticks; a quieter visitor, cherishing his tea bowl, looks from his platform towards the ancient tree. It is blossom time [Plate 78].

The final volume shows the rooms and platforms of a peaceful restaurant beside a fast river. Two men are enjoying the ancient pastime of floating cups of *sake*, one to another, downstream. We view five rooms, where men in various phases of relaxation rest, chat, smoke, drink, eat and prepare tea—no women visible. Mists half-hide the tiled roof and touch a willow tree [Plate 79].

Social life and conversation pieces abound in this guide to the famous places, adding their aspect of truth, for nobody is likely to visit such sights without weaving

Plate 78 (following pages). Miyako Meisho Zue: *A merry picnic*   113

新うすき
去年の蚊の
うすく
桃の花

鬼貫

やうに伏見より大津へ越ゆる
経て大津へらげふよ
道へ秀吉公伏見
沸立城の時より
初し今も関西の
列侯吾妻へ参勤
しぬる人 山を
山道と通る
なる人なを
東海道へ
越きの人

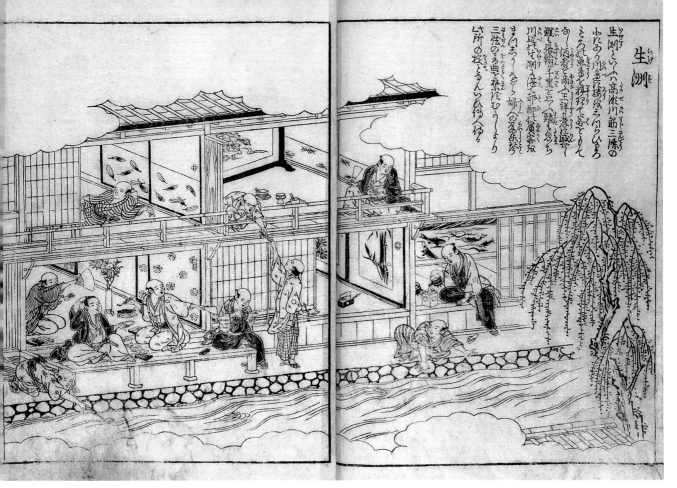

生洲

Plate 79. Miyako Meisho Zue: *Restaurant by the river, Kyoto*

a path among people. They may illustrate the small perception of an ordinary moment—as cameras catch the instant—or poetic beauty; and between those two, who is to judge which represents the "floating world"?

The feudal lord about to travel in his chair over a bridge (Vol. I) is a focus of fuss with his retinue, though two children lean back upon the balustrade in positions which show no hint of respect. The crowd in a shopping street [Plate 80] suggests clearly how it all seemed from the small window of a floor above—in contrast to the formal visit of an aristocrat a few pages later, arriving in his chair at blossom time, greeted by a child and two young women, beside the pillar of a great arch, at the end of an avenue of old trees.

The fourth volume shows several such scenes: arriving in some state at the *ryokan*, where a blossoming tree spreads above the roofs and high wall; carried in his chair along the highway, while a couple of peasants dig the field and stare; strolling in peace along the river path, parasols raised, as the straps of her slipper are adjusted by a maid, mists drift above the fast water and the horse is led forward to a bridge; pausing in a hot day on the steep road one traveller mops his head while the other wipes sweat under his arms. All these take their proper place among famous sights of the Eastern capital.

The next opens with a single-page woodcut: choosing a top or doll, from a stand

116   Plate 80 (following pages). Miyako Meisho Zue: *Shopping street on the hill overlooking Kyoto*

in the street. "Not that," the old woman seems to be saying, "I'll have that over there," pointing beyond the page, while her husband with an infant on his back hunts for the money. In peaceful domesticity husband and wife sit on their verandah to view the sunset (Vol. VI). A family fords the fast stream with some difficulty—

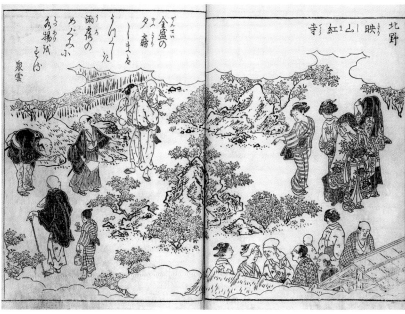

two elderly men riding pick-a-back—as a bamboo cane is held full stretch to help them through. Another, more elegant, fording of the stream is illustrated in the ninth volume, where three ladies decorously lift their kimonos to cross and at the back their servant prepares to follow, after threading all their slippers neatly on a cane.

The large history of blossom-viewing in Japanese art [Plate 81] is not always reflected now in that season, which spreads its junk of black plastic and beer cans under

Plate 81. Miyako Meisho Zue: *Admiring the blossom*

the trees. After many explanations it still remains hard for an Englishman to comprehend the sanctity of plum, tea or cherry as emblems. I was once taken for an enormous, most extravagant taxi ride by a generous scholar in Japan, to a prolific flowering cherry of the kind which is familiar in many of London's front gardens. After minutes of admiration we travelled back.

Plate 82. Miyako Meisho Zue: *Elegance in Kyoto*

The *Miyako Meisho Zue* has its measure of peaceful blossom-viewing scenes [Plate 82]; not only cherry and plum, but bushes of azalea among the rocks—in Shinto belief the spirit of the rocks; kimono patterns echo it in embroidery (Vol. I). A wider scene of high fashion outside and within prosperous homes concludes Volume II: moonlight in a sociable evening, one family watching from an upper verandah, the silhouette through a screen of a woman playing her *samisen* to the

ぬ
の
新
の
塀
ぬ
さ
城
ら
こ
瀧
ゐ
け
る
削
か
け
る
軒
の
住
連
縄

閻
本
萬
福
寺
長
安
寺

元朝寅刻

祇園《ぎをん》

削掛《けづりかけ》

man who is seen as half-silhouette—a characteristic Japanese touch—behind the screen which is drawn half-open to the summer air. Peaceful blossom-viewing on a country path, a servant loaded with the picnic hamper, is illustrated in Volume III; one old man's unashamed aestheticism takes his gaze skywards in adoration. An idyllic cherry-season feast pre-dating black plastic and beer cans appears in Volume VI, where we also find a woman (though sex in these compositions is not always easy to identify) standing on the shoulders of an older man who kneels to support her, tying a paper wish or prayer to the blossoming bough she can just reach. She probably prays for fertility. Two younger men are posed and poised nearby—and, on the ground, is writing-gear which has been put to use.

Meisho-zue could have compared with the camera stops of a Japanese honeymoon but a broader view was taken, a wider lens used, blissful peace balanced by wind, storm and the working day. Vegetable-growers pick their fat *daikon*, carry the heavy

load on a yoke, chat about their merit to a passing couple; to wash roots and leaves in a fast stream, the old woman stands in a wooden protective tub (Vol. I). A boat laden with bundles of wood is pulled powerfully upstream by three—perhaps six—men with ropes on the tow-path, as others watch their labor calmly from a bridge (Vol. I). Rest from wood-carrying, pausing to sit with a pipe, provides a minute's peace though a

Plate 83. Miyako Meisho Zue: *Trouble in a high wind*

couple of clowns mock nearby, while another group continues their journey with formidable loads upon their heads, horses, and shoulders (Vol. V).

Hats are held firm or blow off in a day of wild wind [Plate 83]; melon-cutting is by contrast hot work on a summer day, sweat mopped, lunch-break needed, as a powerful old fellow carries before him by two straps the basket-load of heavy fruit, in labor which must have damaged his back [Plate 84]. Tall baskets of fish, most (not all) covered by cloth against the sun, are carried more wisely across shoulders with yokes, but it looks like painful work; and young women on the path turn

Plate 84. Miyako Meisho Zue: *Cutting melons on a hot day*

away, using fans against the smell (Vol. VII). Near the walls of a shrine, for truth to life, is a study of wind and rain in the street, parasols angled against the storm, children being carried or barefoot and dashing through it.

To leaf among these books with no understanding of text has its own pleasure of half-comprehension, like hearing opera without knowing the story; music explains enough, without words to distract. These illustrations serve as art and mood, with no more need for context. But any account of famous places is inadequate without reference to restaurants, coffee-shops, bakers—Budapest without Gerbo, or Vienna without Sacher. *Miyako Meisho Zue* has its scattering of restaurants at temples and places of natural beauty—and in Volume V, happily, the sweet shop. There it is, a famous establishment with name-brand prominent above, a long front to the street where, as in all good places of the sort, we observe the two cooks hard at work, pounding raw material in a vat before cakes are made and completed for display.

Laid out on two trays we see them, other trays piled at the back, a girl in her kimono fixing ribbons on every box for sale [Plate 85]. This is the place for a few quiet words, or perhaps a quick snack in passing. Decorum prevails, greed exists.

In visiting this book, as in viewing such a place, it is easy to neglect the roofs and parks, water, bridges and trees, in the pleasure of life or work perceived, manners, weather, the passing moment. This has become a

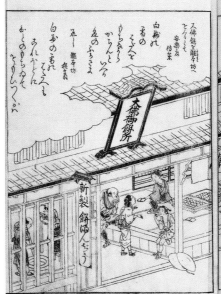

Plate 85. Miyako Meisho Zue: *The sweet shop, Kyoto*

habit of mind, for as no city now bears these qualities so the traveller seeks this or that "ancient monument" or spot worth seeing. The merit of *meisho-zue* is that we realize it was all worth seeing, and all was shown.

To travel through the many volumes of Hasegawa Settan's *Edo Meisho Zue* from fifty years on, in similar spirit, would be otiose in this book, but the journey is recommended. Settan is described in Laurence Roberts's dictionary as an Ukiyo-e printmaker and illustrator, "particularly well known for his illustrations in *Edo Meisho Zue*" [Plates 86 & 87]. These are legion, in this work of twenty volumes which appeared between 1834 and 1836.

When I first brought this home, scribbling an enthusiastic note I called it "a prodigious and most miraculous work, a kind of poetic Microcosm of Tokyo. It is so much more than a guide book: the almost unbelievable number of woodcuts give us the manifold moods, places, activities, scenes of the old Edo which so few Westerners ever visited. We have a strong impression from it of coherence, of everything to scale as one might expect; with a most surprising variety from dense crowd to scenes of the deepest peace. If the first purpose was to show street plans, the layout of the city where the temples, palaces and commercial quarters lay, then of course the need is supplied here; but it seems every facet of life comes along with it, the markets and tea houses, the restaurants, street stalls, ordinary scenes of passing day, sports, children, admiration of the blossom, processions, theater and the outlying areas of rural peace. As woodcut it is an astounding work of course, the compositions always careful and the panoramas in the lightest lines giving us invariably a certain artistic angle of approach with a constant fascination for the pattern of roof and street."

Compared with the Kyoto work from fifty years before, here is lighter line and more dense composition. After nearly two and a half centuries of Tokugawa rule, Edo—Tokyo—had become a crowded focus of life, from temple to shopping-street and fishmarket, teeming with people, boats, commerce, shrines. Settan's lighter line allowed him to convey this sense of an ant-heap capital, alive and in scale. Here are the city and its surroundings unchanged in style towards the close of the

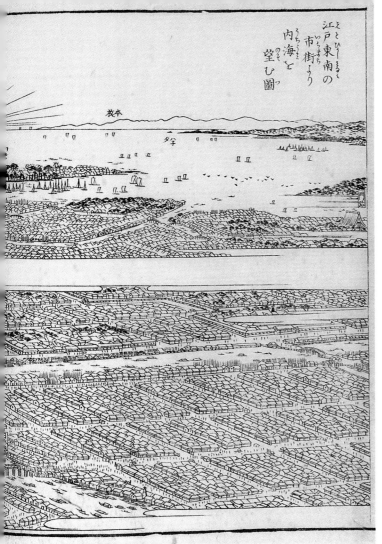

Plate 86. Edo Meisho Zue: *Tokyo in the late Edo period*

long period of isolation. Thronged streets were the wonder of that world: life itself, Tokyo 1830, boats on the Sumida river, many waterways before a brutish overhead road system darkened and polluted them. One wonders at the artist's ability to handle so many different kinds of scene.

Everybody knows how cramped and harsh were, and to some extent still are, the circumstances of those lives; yet the place was always visually marvellous, within or beyond—and people poured out to view it, were conscious of it, grew to a sense of that taste. In days of such beauty, changing with the seasons, home poverty and hard work saw enough delight to balance modern prosperity, which confines poetic vision to small pockets of sentiment or a few shrines and parks. From these illustrations we understand very well that people blessed their environment, recognized their luck, accepted proper compensation for a rough passage.

The first scenic woodcut in Volume I gives the mood: an "artist's impression," as it would now be called, of Tokyo's jam-packed roofs, little dwellings below a mighty rising sun; figures crowding the streets, boats on every waterway, total density of habitation [Plate 86]. Coming into close focus, crowds cross one of the bridges and we see most boats are laden with bundles or barrels. Warehouses, shops, stalls abound, the whole area teems with life—within conventional borders of cloud which provide white space for a caption. And the bridge is delicately built, between customary banks of jig-saw stone.

Advancing further we recognize from a century and a half ago Tsukiji, the fish-market. Visitors to Tokyo are wise to get up intolerably early and catch the first train to Tsukiji, scene of high tension as trolleys and tractors menace each path, *alfresco* auctions generate extremes of excitement and families in their booths sort out the fish or perform their surgery and arrange it like flowers. Much has changed, as one views the woodcut, but not all: there is the auctioneer impressing his group;

porters, before the help and smell of tractors, carry on long yokes their basket-burdens of fish; somebody presides with a big account-book; the tuna are prominent, whole or dismembered; boats arrive for immediate unloading. No doubt off-stage were the sushi bars, with food, rest and *sake* available after hard work.

Total contrast, still in Volume I, is in the calm printseller's shop, a wide double-fronted decorous place where varied activities of that art take place [Plate 87]. Piles of sheets occupy a platform on the tatami waiting to be folded, stitched, bound as books; others are made into albums, or mounted as folding screens. Two young women view them with pleasure, while other connoisseurs examine examples of actor-prints. Life passes through this civilized street, a woman carried in her chair by four servants, preceded by two others with luggage on their backs. All are well-dressed; kites fly in the breeze above, a pet dog rests.

Plate 87. Edo Meisho Zue: The publisher's shop, Edo

Timeless pleasures took their place with streets and markets among the famous scenes of Tokyo: picnicking on a platform, for instance, to watch the sunset. Most of a page is given to formal trees, hills, stone shrines, a suggestion of rice fields below; but up steep steps and beside a well-disciplined hedge friends take supper; under the trees, on a mound or hill, above the plain; seated, gesturing; animated talk, in conditions of peace. An arch to the extreme right shows they are just outside the approach to a temple.

Women in formal dress greet the spring, wander through a park, while others nearby show devotion to the moment: talking, visiting a flowering magnolia. A comparatively harsh scene across two pages shows one pitiless old man dragging his child up a path by moonlight in winter, both of them dressed with some formality; as if she were an unwilling child-bride, in this harmony of bamboo, water and willow. The tranquillity of a simpler couple among peonies and lilies, with plants in pots, as she fills the wash-tub and he sits on a bamboo bench with his fan and tea-bowl, looking across to the cultivation of a neighboring garden, conveys untroubled domestic peace from those days.

If social realism seems now opposed to quiet in the countryside, or street pleasures of a city, this work serves to remind us that they co-existed; for its merit is factual as a map, without hint or need of propaganda. Luckily, publishers had the wit to engage artists who took the occasion of their large commissions to record the spectrum of life among people and hills, work, shrines and the street. Nostalgia had not yet arrived; that was not their approach, though it may be ours now as we leaf through what they bequeathed.

*   *   *   *   *

WITHIN the same scope but conceived in a different way are the five volumes of *Nikko San Shi* ("Outline of the Mountains of Nikko") produced in 1837 but prepared across a number of years before that [Plate 88]. Nikko is no further from Tokyo than Stratford from London, but Japanese holiday traffic is such that I have turned back rather than fight to arrive. The beauty of its waterfalls among mountains and temples is undiminished since that book appeared. It was then, and remains, a place of pilgrimage as the monument to Ieyasu and the era he inaugurated. One climbs paths among brightly decorative shrines, to his tomb. In the hills above is a series of waterfalls, which spirits inhabit.

Hillier remarks that "because of the shogunal family connections" this work "was produced with unusual reverence and splendour . . . leading masters of Kano, Nanga, Shijo and Ukiyo-e give a rich and diverse series of pictures, cut and printed with great care." Among the artists working thus in their varied styles were

Plate 88. Nikko San Shi: Mountain and waterfall

Hokusai, Buncho and Chinnen. On the principle that things good in themselves are also good neighbors to each other, there was no need for other unity in design. We see temples as in the Kyoto and Edo books, and Nikko as a small town among mountains, no crowds filling the streets and (contrasting with present-day Nikko) no shops. Priests overwhelmed in reverence bow to the spirits of the Taki-no-O waterfall, in an illustration signed by Chinnen. A lively picnicking scene, tea made and lunch boxes open, under the pines with a mountain view, might be here or at any comparable spot in Japan, but most subjects are more mystic with waterfalls, ceremonies, the spirit of the place assumed or manifest, difference in the style of art expressing private visions of religious experience. This Nikko book becomes a display of Japanese impressions in black and white—the Kegon waterfall, by Buncho, opens Volume IV with emphatic vigor—with an additional contrast of several quite literal illustrations of birds and plants, color-printed. As a technical performance in woodcut and printing it stands high, surprising any eye with a panorama of rock and water across four pages by Hokusai. It improves with each encounter.

The close of Volume IV is characteristic: a double-page in purest Shijo-cockney manner by Mori Ippo ("Separating copper particles by washing"), followed at once by a simple panorama of villages, hills and temples; then the powerful realism of miners at work in their passage through darkness; next the lightest line-impression of mountain rock, as two travellers cross a plank bridge above high waterfalls. And the final volume, after comparable contrasts, ends with two clowns hopping on stilts ("Ceremonial dancers," says Mitchell's bibliography, accurately perhaps). As an introduction to artists, woodcutters and printers towards the fine close of a tradition, *Nikko San Shi* combines many aspects in a marvellous performance.

*   *   *   *   *

AN early twentieth century example of *meisho-zue* has attracted some attention recently. C.H. Mitchell's contribution to a volume of essays on Japanese art in honor of Jack Hillier (1982) was called "*Hanshin Meisho Zue*, a Little-Known Early Shin Hanga Series" (*shin*=new; *han*=woodcut). Hillier has also written about it in his *Art of the Japanese Book*. This modern flowering of an old plant, published by Bun'endo in Tokyo in 1916, consists of thirty color-prints with title-page (which includes a map) and list of contents. It is a map of the Osaka and Kobe area; the book's title means "Views of Famous Places around Osaka and Kobe."

Bun'endo was responsible for several fine productions. "It is said," wrote Mitchell, "that he seldom criticized his authors or editors, but he spent much time chivvying the artisans who turned out his books, insisting on very high standards. In fact, he

Plate 89. From Hanshin Meisho Zue, *1916*

constantly faced bankruptcy because of high operating costs." For the standards he achieved one must now be grateful in viewing these thirty prints, which are all described and attributed in Mitchell's essay. Five artists provided the drawings. "The outstanding block-cutter of the time," Hillier writes, "Igami Bonkotsu, was frequently responsible for the prints in Bun'endo's books."

The combination of artists within one work was time-honored, less surprising here than in the Nikko volumes where range and style produced amusing contrast. These five in 1916 represented a moment when the artist's eye in Japan, at home in its own tradition, had learned the fashions and phases of Western painting. Hillier writes of one of the prints that it "has such strong Western elements that we are reminded not so much of earlier Japanese landscape prints as of prints by Western masters who adopted the Japanese techniques of print-making." Or of drawing, or painting.

Hanshin Meisho Zue represents the form in a half-way pause between Japanese and Western art [Plate 89]. If we have heard enough of *japonisme*, here is the other side of the story. Old vision is present in the impressions of trees, or composition of landscape—yet this is an artists' work concerned with scene more than with life. People are there incidentally, because people occur, but not closely observed (with one exception, where a visiting Western family with luggage by the quay is perceived as irritatingly stupid). Wit and joy give way to placid observation of disappearing Japan. The thirty prints with preliminary leaves were issued separately in their day, or bound as a book. My set was joined (but not mounted) as a long scroll or *emaki*, the new age traditionally housed. If colors were different and startling, paper more luxurious, nothing in the old skills of grey shading among mists, trees, or the use of wood-grain, had disappeared. Color and art replace the level survey of temple, hill, street, picnic and market-place. One misses the gossip, and evidence of *sake*.

*   *   *   *   *

GUIDE BOOKS suggest travel—forbidden or restricted under the Tokugawa regime, but curious minds made their own exceptions. Shiba Kokan, who lived from 1747 to 1818, was just such an independent spirit: wanderer, recording in sketchbooks whatever intrigued him, explorer in art as well as geography, the first to practice metal engraving in Japan. Upon his maps of the world on two sheets, in the late eighteenth century, he declared they were copper-engraved by the pioneer of that method in Japan. His oil-painting, "Picture of the seven-league beach at Kamakura in Soshu," stood out from others at the Great Japan Exhibition in London, 1981, as an example of topographical art in the Western manner, recalling perhaps the work of Hodges, Chinnery or Thomas Daniell. The catalogue for that exhibition described him thus:

> Kokan was a leading student of western mathematics and science, as well as an artist who could paint in Japanese Ukiyo-e style, who studied Chinese painting at Nagasaki, designed for popular wood-block prints and did copper-plate etchings and engravings in the European manner. He also made many attempts to copy European styles of art, especially oil painting, and his admiration for them led him to an unreasonable contempt for the art traditions of Japan.

There is no evidence of that contempt in the "Account of Western Travels" (*Seiyu Ryotan*) published in 1794 and again in 1803; the "Western" of his title being of course western Japan, as far as the privileged Dutch trading center at Nagasaki which offered enough material for his curiosity.

These five volumes record whatever interested Kokan during that journey, in a text amply illustrated with black-and-white woodcuts taken from his sketchbooks. Like a lesser Hokusai, everything intrigued him: plants, small bays and boats, ceremony and peasant dance, the way villages were perched above a precipice or a long bridge spanned the water. His trees and landscape were sketched in the Chinese (Nanga) style, a tradition constantly absorbed by artists in Japan; here is nothing Western, or copper-engraved. To have made such a journey was adventure enough.

Small sketches of wooded slope, rock and bay are lively, spontaneous within their style, as he travelled past views of Fuji among snows and mist; city roofs, shrines, memorial stones in rows like chess pawns interested him also; but he was deeply fascinated by the whalers at Misaki, and Dutch at Nagasaki.

Whaling he approached by way of other fisheries, observing boats as they sailed among rocks and pools of an inlet to the open sea, past small steep islands where steps climbed high to cottages and a shrine. He sketches the trawl net, and we see how half-a-dozen boats surround it to heave in their alarming catch of a tuna shoal, while a whale blows its spray above the horizon. Later in this same fourth volume they attack the whale, a combined operation, and beach it. Safe on shore, ropes attached by capstan, petty men mount and flay it, carry away flesh on yokes and shoulders. Across two pages we see the great factory where these blocks of flesh become food in barrels, or oil from flames of a multiple furnace. A worker is searched for anything precious he may have hidden among his clothes.

If this now seems sad work, we turn back with pleasure to Nagasaki, the crowded port, where fields cover hills and a great Dutch ship is at anchor in the bay. That was a focus of highest interest, for Shiba Kokan. On deck astern, under an awning, three merchants discuss their affairs in conditions of comfort. The design of this large boat intrigues him, as does the layout of Deshima itself: the small Dutch settlement, a walled village, where an unwilling cow is dragged along to be slaughtered, presumably. No less interesting than the place are its people, their lives and deaths: sailors in the rigging or, high across the spectrum but at ground level, the thoroughly comfortable sitting room of a Dutch merchant—all very amazing, chairbacks and spittoons, table and decanters, portraits hanging, chandelier, barometer. Arranged along two shelves are folio volumes of uniform height—accounts, ledgers, beyond question. It is a trader's room, with portraits from home and of the ship he owns.

Another ship is shown in the day's work, local boats crowding alongside, fetching and carrying, selling. Scenes of the wide harbor and its islands conclude with graveyard ceremonies and the conspicuous Dutch tomb, under a canopy, of R. KOOP, cut in that Japanese style of European lettering which is familiar to this day.

It is easy to guess why bridges among the islands and rocks or steps to almost unapproachable places fascinated Shiba Kokan—became emblems in this charming book which reached across civilizations.

*   *   *   *   *

A DIFFERENT tradition from that of Shiba Kokan produced still more remarkable results. Travel, even within Japan, was forbidden; voyages overseas within the bounds of trade were necessary, but now and then in Japan as anywhere else and at any time anarchy asserts itself. Sailors tend to cherish a certain independence, are less likely than many other workers to conform; for long periods they occupy a private world, and develop it. If Japanese sailors suffered shipwreck it was their duty to return home at once, but shipwrecked sailors had a way of showing a natural curiosity about the places where they were cast ashore. Occasional "shipwreck" for the sailors had something in common with "going sick" among employees of a modern organization.

More often than not it happened at Kamchatka, the extreme eastern part of the Russian Empire. Quite plausible, to put into Kamchatka awhile for repairs, and pleasant to suffer some delay before returning; but four sailors in the last decade of the eighteenth century took greatly extended leave after finding themselves ashore upon that island near Alaska.

After a period at Kamchatka, mutually agreeable it seems, they resolved to settle rather than follow their duty in making a belated return home; but their presence was reported to the Tsar, who had never seen travellers from Japan. He ordered them to Moscow, a colossal journey, where they were engaged as tutors in the Japanese language. There can never have been a stranger language school with less qualification for teaching, even at the fringes of Oxford in vacation, than was founded by these shipwrecked sailors from northern Honshu. However, after serving two years in Moscow, founding their school, these adventurers gained permission to continue their journey west (east was likely to produce severe penalty). They came to England, crossed the Atlantic, and made their way home at last, the first Japanese explorers to have travelled round the world.

Arriving back they expected to be cast into prison, but with such an extraordinary story to tell they received lenient treatment and nominal punishment, settling sensibly then to record their report. As the whole affair was highly illegal, irregular, improper, it could not be published—but the text, by them or "as told to . . .," circulated in manuscript, with illustrations in color [Plates 90 & 91]. In seven volumes, it must have become well known; several examples are recorded, one is beside me now. I have seen another for sale in Japan and a third in an American university library. Yet it could not be printed until the Meiji period in Japan, about a century after the voyage was completed. A reduced version has been issued in Germany, with no attempt to reproduce the illustrations in character; it has never been translated into English. The chance exists, for an enterprising publisher.

In looking through these seven volumes which probably date from four decades after the voyage was completed, and are copied from copies of hearsay, one finds a natural mix of fable and close-to-truth. The naked woman with a man whose entire skin is covered in paint or tattoo, both of them with scarlet lips, could pass for truth except that they both have clawed feet and his head sprouts two horns. In the same volume is a pleasant double-page drawing of the harbor, where perhaps the voyagers lived, with boats and hills and conifers; preceded by another, less likely to be true, recalling the owl and the pussycat, of a second horned and patterned couple, guiding their raft which rests upon the flat back of a sea-monster.

Birds, botany and sea-beasts are illustrated from time to time, as are dress and house-construction. The paper was given a mica-dust surface to receive these water-color drawings. The woman with beads hanging from her ears and nose is followed by sketches of nose and ear which explain just how they fitted. Eskimos hunt a large fish from their kayak; the next pages show such a kayak for two, another for three people, the hand-grip for their arrow, and hunting dress. Home is illustrated after that, a family clothed cheerfully, fashionably, entering thick walls down a flight of steps.

This northern volume has a fine double-page of a tall ship, Chinese it seems (from the sailors' hats), all sails set, navigating among bare snow-covered rocks. Horses and harness were of equal interest. A fully-enclosed sleigh with bell and prancing ponies slides its way across two pages west, towards domestic comfort. The intelligent diagram of a stove brings news of how it worked; chairs, carved and turned, are the essence of elegant life. This volume closes with the gable-end of a

Plate 90 (following pages). "Castaway" manuscript: The balloon ascent

well built Western house, smoke shooting up from its chimney, front door open to a flight of stairs, someone under another porch warming himself by the flames, no door visible to protect his back. The final opening apparently illustrates, luxury of luxuries, a sauna, with benches rising as in theaters, while a well-dressed servant stokes the flames backstage.

Boats and flags follow, and a warship, guns directed through every porthole. As a blockhouse above the sea is also illustrated, one may feel surprised that these sailors were received in Moscow to open their language school, rather than executed in Siberia for spying. Soldiers in full uniform with colored coats and crimson linings, brass buttons, busbies, pikes, intrigued them of course and are illustrated in series. Back to the port again, we see how capstans were used from shore to pull in the great net for fish—as Shiba Kokan had observed, in his journey through the west of Japan. A tall open-sided structure by the sea is shown, among trees and below a waterfall; apparently a weaving workshop, where the cloth could also be washed and, as we see from the man who approaches with what looks like an outsize surf-board, dried in the sun.

As they travel further from snow into summer we see a coach-and-six, running upon three wheels. In paler colors but of stronger interest perhaps is the miller at work in his windmill, pouring corn into the hopper beside four open sacks of flour.

A climax of astonishment marks their approach to the capital. Fork, knife and spoon are illustrated as emblems of civility. Shirts, tunics, embroidered collars, the pattern and tassels of a shawl are shown in such detail as a tailor could imitate. The belfry of a church, below its Russian Orthodox cross, is followed by the hard-worked but well-dressed bellringer who needs both hands and a foot for his noisy art. We approach a great cathedral—and, in one of the dramatic illustrations, enter it. Something of the awe with which they first saw such a mighty place, its arches and spaces, filters to this repetition of a report. Then—a puzzle—we find another impressive device which looks like living people in five large open-air television screens attached by curving red pipes to a central stronghold. This can only have been a fairground scene, amazing on first glance as any cathedral, while visitors in their boxes slung on the red poles gyrated and no doubt, then as now, felt sick. Several less adventurous wanderers observe them.

Two final volumes introduce marvels and surprises of the capital, to which we are led symbolically by a full-dress guard of honor presenting arms: long green coats red-lined, busbies, bayonets drawn. With practical curiosity the next impression is of a fire-engine, drawn with its thick grey hoses for reception and supply, wooden wheels, handles for two men to push and lift for a constant jet. Coinage is illustrated, musical instruments (dulcimer, viola da gamba and its bow,

Plate 91. "Castaway" manuscript: Skyscrapers

flute), a snarling otter rather vaguely remembered.

High glory arrives in the last volume with facing portraits of the Tsar and Tsarina seen large and close in full formal dress—perhaps in their box at the opera, to which a visit was made. Next page shows a balloon ascent [Plate 90], two passengers in the decorative basket, the balloon (striped as they still are) held down by six ropes manually, a gaily colored scene; then we view it risen above the sea, as a family group waves and wonders, and one boy watches through his telescope. This section closes with scientific miracles of an observatory where one could view, a vast globe, from ground level or a balcony: and the platform from which people observed, through domed glass, the night sky. Vauxhall and Ranalagh had nothing to rival these, which look more like present-day Texas than eighteenth-century Russia.

A few random surprises remain, among them a clear impression of densely-built, seven-story blocks of flats seen from above, with little people in the street; and chimneys, which must have provided a form of central heating, sending up jets of smoke [Plate 91]. A monastery rises through conventional mist in the distance. A large flower shop or botanical forcing-house claims one double-page illustration, pot-plants displayed at five levels of shelving—interesting because of the heating system, assisted by a series of solar panels in the roof. More glamorous was a full-dress opera performance, musicians spaced along the front stage, a mighty chandelier, two singers performing, an audience of women and children below the balcony or perched on steps.

After an equestrian statue facing and pointing out to sea, the most surprising sight shows four drinkers seated round a large table, conversationally with bowls and bottles; for standing on its crimson cloth, in full formal dress, is a dwarf. Such was a sad entertainment of those days. One more earnest illustration of harbor defenses, with ships and forts and blockhouses, concludes the work.

No doubt the incredible journey of these sailors from Japan will appear one day in an English edition, and receive wider recognition.

*   *   *   *   *

WE should return to the early-Meiji phrase books, where this journey began. They flowed from that release of energy which came with freedom to accept the West, to listen and explore. Phrase-books, in a simple tradition of Japanese publishing, helped the business clerks, the shopkeepers and semi-educated. It was mentioned that a different style appeared in a confident little volume with picture cover, *Convenient Book for English*, produced in Osaka by a bookseller-publisher called Aoki Suzando. He turns up now, self-assured and adventurous, with two appealing series of guides: *Illustrated Guide Book for Travellers Around Japan* (seven volumes) and *Illustrated Guide Book for Travellers Round the World* (seven volumes and a world map). Both sets continued the tradition of *meisho-zue*.

Aoki Suzando was seizing bulls by their horns. As travel within Japan had been restricted for three centuries, and travel abroad forbidden, these represented the new freedom. They combine charm with taste and a fine vagueness about that obsession of modern publishers, "the market." As book-production they jump into more popular format, with color-printed pictures over boards to bind them; the oddity which makes some account possible here is English captions, erratic and fearless, to the many hundred illustrations which adorn the Japanese text. One wonders about the thought behind those captions: in Japan were they for the tour-guide to show his visitor—or in the world, for Japanese travellers to show their guides? Neither of these, perhaps; just a venture over the border into Western habit.

They are excellent little books to leaf through; and if in a journey you get quickly bored (as I do) with information the text in Japanese is an advantage. Technically too they joined West with East. A new method was used for illustration: relief metal-cut like white-line wood engraving—Bewick's technique—difficult and delicate to manage, practical in Japan for just a few years in the last quarter of the century. Paper suitable for such fine-line reproduction, smooth, machine-made, was folded at the fore-edges in the traditional Japanese way. End-leaves and all edges were marbled, an innovation for which, as has been mentioned, these books are now admired by collectors in Japan. Varied coloring upon title pages gives a well-planned surprise in each volume; English display lettering is a mix of Victorian and a popular notion of Western-Japanese as in programs and posters for Gilbert and Sullivan's *Mikado*.

Yet one is astonished most by this frontal attack upon a large area of ignorance, recalling the suggested letter (already quoted) in Aoki's *Convenient Book for English*, which begins:

> "Dear Sir,
>
> During my last visit to your house, you were pleased to call my attention to a book entitled 'Illustrated guide book for travellers round the world' which I remember to have been a work of so much interest, that I feel inclined to peruse it. . ."

So confident, he was unlikely to fail.

Superficially some comparison with Baedecker springs to mind, but any closer connection with that earnest and unerring companion would indeed be false. For the round-the-world tour it is certain that neither Aoki nor his staff were travellers; most probably what is now called "picture-research" dredged up a high percentage of what we see in the metal cuts—from such sources as the *Illustrated London News*—and a pleasing proportion of the rest was pure imagination. Biblical and historical scenes appear, copied from easy sources. The engravers imitated very ably in this new technique, as they had in the old. Scenes could be understood, needed no translation and minimal interpretation; captions in English offered another problem. Sometimes quite a difficult caption was perfectly transferred—for instance, "View of the Ephesian Temple of Diana," or "Interior Scene of Judicial Court, Baroda." Several craftsmen, equal and less equal to the task, were at work. All these little books provide an agreeable mixture of ingenuity, art, success and failure, fact and fancy. Difficulties were overcome by making the attempt.

Volume I, with no clear regard for priorities, travels from New York to Niagara, and Cape Horn, with a glance at Honolulu and Tokyo. Two excellent early illustrations show sights which may truly have impressed a returning traveller: New York's smart new "elevated rail road," now quite gone but lingering as a sordid memory for survivors who knew it, and across two full pages "The Interior View of Patent House, Washington." The Patent House appears three times before this volume ends; somebody must have seen it, and been overwhelmed. In the last pages Aoki advertises his around-Japan series of guides.

Volumes II and III, less distinguished in production, thinner than the others, cope barely with Western Europe—opening with a volvelle, "The Table of Hour of the Situation of Every Cities Around the World," more attractive than is now seen in hotel lobbies, and attached by a neat knot of silk. Capital cities are interesting, though grey and idiosyncratic; capital letters, in which the captions are cut, gave trouble. There was a sharp difference between efficient copying, in preparing these captions, and the transcription of oral notes—for example, in the heading which must have begun its journey from Edinburgh as "View from Arthur's Seat," but arrived in Osaka as VIEWFROM ARSASSIETE HILL. The Parisian section shows two familiar instances of L for R, which remain a difficulty for Japanese students of English, above illustrations called PALAIS LOYAL, and CHURCH OF NOTELARDM.

Volume IV has more of Western Europe, but we go there (as planes do now) via the Arctic; its cover shows a fiery sunset behind icebergs, two ships in the sound, polar bears and penguins, while two reindeer with fine antlers prance across ice-floes pulling a well-wrapped-up Eskimo in his sleigh. In these wilder shores of the imagination a few captions lose touch with comprehension. NATIV KILL THE GREAT BEAR VITH ANY DECEPTION we read, and see in the forest below it a large bear, paw on the shoulder of a manly Russian who seems to spike the poor creature with a back-handed movement of his wrist. The scene is neither pleasant nor explicit, but had its source perhaps in someone's tall story. FALL DOWN ICE PIECE ON WINTER is a successfully descriptive phrase for total snow and far-northern desolation. Less successful, though overcoming the customary mistake, to describe a museum exhibit, is THE PUTRIFIED MAN.

The fifth volume, covering Africa and Australia (including excellent metal cuts of Cairo) has the largest, wildest mingling of supposition. This was such stuff as dreams are made of, irresistible, as for instance across two pages near the start: A PHIPOPOTAMOS MUNCHES NATIVES WITH A RAFT. Africa was the place where alarming things happened. CROCODILE MUNCHES NATIVES AND AN OX we see later, and there he is, poor fellow, all limbs still intact as the crocodile makes for shore. The picture of two naked Africans tumbling in alarm before a towering open-jawed reptile is called BOA PURSUE AFTER NATIVES. "Natives" and slaves called forth constant fascination.

Three forms of easily comprehended misunderstanding occur in this volume: mis-spelling, mis-pronunciation, and misapprehension. One letter transposed produces a curious result, below the caption PICTURE OF WATERSPOTUS: there it is, rising like a nightmare beast from the sea to digest little ships down its long neck into the depth. The wrong pronunciation shows INHABITANTS OF USTRARIA—descending to us in dialect which is still familiar.

The misapprehensions arose in quite another way: some member of Aoki's staff knew two things about camels—they inhabit Africa, and have long necks. Leafing through his reference pictures he found what seemed to fit the need and prepared two illustrations, one called CAMELUS BEGATS EGGS, the other (across two pages) FEEDING CAMELAS IN THE GREAT FIELD. He had of course come upon an article about the ostrich, for camels do not lay eggs, have beaks or grow feathers. The Boer farmer is faithfully shown, at his farm on the high veldt, boxing eggs and sorting chicks. This was the period of prosperity for him, when fashionable hats needed ostrich feathers.

The sixth volume takes us to India (FIERCE TIGERS HURTS TRAVEL-LARS). In the final volume, no doubt well-informed and first-hand, we travel via the Malay peninsula, SINGAPOLE and Burma to China where English captions were reckoned unnecessary. This successful adventure in publishing ends with a folded map of the world, color-printed, copied from a European example: Britain is central, Japan far out to the right. Japanese map-makers soon appreciated that their own land could occupy a focal place, shoving Western Europe out to the left-hand margin.

Aoki produced his seven volumes of *Illustrated Guide Books for Travellers Around Japan* in just the same ways as the world series with bilingual titles, English captions and Japanese text. They provide, in that difficult technique of relief-metal cuts, tempting glimpses of all manner of scene and aspect of life, on the eve of change. With every sympathetic grimace towards the modern Japanese city, kind though one tries to feel about change, I realize flicking through these illustrations of Japan when the scale was human, that the urban scene has become beyond doubt or a questioning moment visually atrocious. How strange the "View of Nihonbashi" when traffic was a mingling of rickshaws and horse-drawn trams, by the two-story houses with tiled and gabled roofs. People in Western clothes were not necessarily visitors, for Western dress had become fashionable.

Though many of the illustrations are undistinguished, similar to the average style of missionary textbook in that period, they convey their proper impression from more than a century ago. Temples and shrines remain for us still, havens of peace afflicted by minimal plastic. Much is recognizable, apart from scenery, through all the change. These pictures summon ghosts, as musicians can. Photography and foreign books brought natural imitation, different perspective; there is almost nothing to connect these stylistically with the *meisho-zue* of a century before; yet one is never in doubt that the artists and engravers were Japanese. Aoki had not imported Western draughtsmen.

Bays, bridges, hills, hot-springs, shrines, waterfalls, cities are here, with much Western dress and the presence of telegraph wires. A panorama of flat fields, not obviously different from others, has the menacing caption "View of the Improving Work." On the whole, these volumes give our last view of unimproved Japan.

There is little provision for an English reader except, by surprise, one full page near the start of Volume III, THE HOT SPRINGS OF HAKONE. Nearest to Tokyo, much visited then as now, it is still fun to take the funicular railway, enter the cable car, swing across a patch of wild mountain and hot sulphur, pause for an egg cooked in its fumes, and find oneself down by lake Ashi with the famous view—if by some rare chance mist does not hide it—of Fuji.

> The spring is the charming with the lark's song of wellcome in the morning, followed by the anther of many birds, until the hototogisn sings his good night song to the moon-night.

Next year I shall be there again, and can hardly wait.

CHAPTER TEN
A POSTSCRIPT ON MAPS

Though ignorance of scientific map-reading should be a deterrent, some postscript to *meisho-ki*, on this highly visual subject, is needed. Certain styles prevailed from early periods; as in the related theme of travel, there was something short of curiosity and accuracy in the Japanese approach to maps. If the modern tourist seeks help in guide books, for identifying a temple or following a route, some form of schematic sketch may be easiest to understand; such was often one kind of map-making in Japan. An instinctive ability to convey the practical, rather than the accurate, connects the earliest "Gyogi-style" maps with a modern tourist pamphlet, boards in parks, and directions scribbled by a hotel porter for the taxi driver.

If the Japanese were late in achieving geographic accuracy, it was perhaps one result of a closed society and long-lasting indifference to exploration. Indian origins of Buddhism, with jealous curiosity about the civilization of China and Korea, formed the philosophical borders of their world. "Very few maps are still in existence," we read, "from before the middle of the sixteenth century," and nothing near to accuracy until much later than that. A division prevailed between maps of the world—wildly ignorant until European examples leaked in—and surveys of Japan, which served their purposes but kept their distance from scientific survey. Both kinds, in varying styles, are visually very beautiful.

Those maps which show a curious affinity with modern notice-boards in public

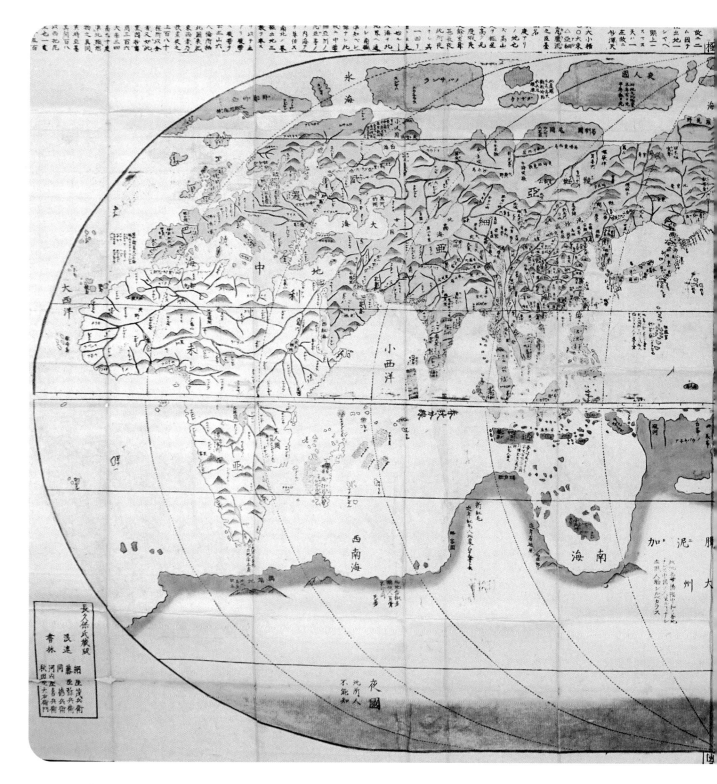

parks were the earliest, attributed to a monk called Gyogi who lived from 668 to 749. A scheme of outline loops showing land ownership and boundaries characterized this form of map-making, in response to the governing need for feudal information. Examples of such estate surveys survive from the Nara period—legible, informative, unrelated to other aspects of accuracy. These cadastral maps

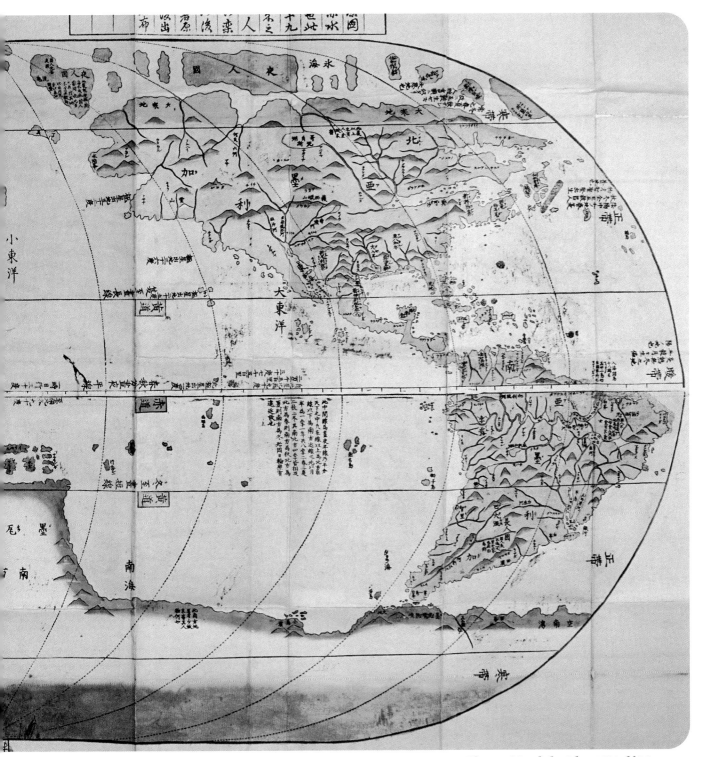

Plate 92. Nagakubo Sekisui: World Map, 1785

("*a survey on a scale sufficiently large to show accurately the extent and measurement of every field and other plot of land*"—OED) exist in the Shoso-in, and are shown upon occasion at Nara. The connection with modern tourist equipment is not surprising, for a tradition of Gyogi-style maps continued into the nineteenth century.

A different tradition, in response to practical need, has much in common with the old Japanese skill of viewing scenes as if the artist were poised above them, mentioned earlier as characteristic of the Tosa style or *Yamato-e* which simply means Japanese picture; commonly found in picture scrolls and the domestic scenes of *Nara-ehon*. These panoramic maps show mountains, cities, rivers as in aerial photography; and as the map-makers could not fly, it remains a mysteriously wonderful form of art. Hokusai was responsible for such a map of the Kiso-ji road in 1819, Keisai for another of Japan at about the same time. These woodcuts from artists whose work was not chiefly concerned with maps are not astonishing in a subject which often lay nearer to art than geography; the continuing Gyogi style is appealing in its loyalty to a valid tradition. Schematic loops of information rather than shape continued well into the nineteenth century, as did the fascinating "Buddhist" world maps, quite unrelated to knowledge of the world's existence as shapes of land and sea. This seeming vagueness was not a symptom of indifference: maps were drawn on elegant fans, or engraved decoratively on the backs of ancient mirrors, upon *inro, netsuke* and sword guards. Maps were a delight.

A persistence of Buddhist world maps expresses perennial division of mind between religious and literal truth, as in our own thought and language. These are maps of the Buddhist world, or "the Five Indies;" a famous example exists at the Horyu-ji in Nara. As Sir Hugh Cortazzi describes it, "The Himalayas are shown as snow-capped peaks in the centre of the map, and Mt. Sumeru, the mythical centre of the cosmos, is depicted in a whirlpool-like form." Comparable maps were made until the late Edo period, into Victorian times, including such up-to-the-minute decorations as a large trading ship and a striped balloon or airship. Such maps of the mind held their place alongside investigations into the true measure of longitude, representing facets of truth which could and can co-exist.

Another convention which resolved itself slowly was the placing of North, which we suppose to lie above South. It has been suggested that as Japanese maps were generally spread on the floor, seen from all angles by those who gathered round, there was no particular reason to draw North on top. That argument could be specious, for Western maps may have been used by groups sitting around tables more often than hung on walls, and Japanese people could lift their maps. The dubious need for practical accuracy was perhaps a historic reason.

Unrelated to accuracy but eloquent in other ways, when European maps arrived for imitation—William Adams is known to have advised Ieyasu, and would certainly have shown a map—the Japanese long continued the custom of placing their country far east, at the edge. By whatever truth exists in the East-West concept there was nothing against occupying middle space on world maps, which Dutch and Portuguese cartographers had seized for themselves. Japan eventually became the central concept upon Japanese maps of the world, as did India upon Buddhist maps.

Projection offered another dilemma, which the scientists solved or accepted when Western notions were allowed to enter and replace an early Confucian concept. Shiba Kokan at the end of the eighteenth century published, with his world map, a text explaining and expounding the Copernican system. In the early seventeenth century and even before, when traders and missions began to introduce their practical knowledge of these matters, large maps on six-fold and eight-fold screens, which survive, must have been the pride and joy of those privileged at court or in castles who were allowed to see them. The Jotoku-ji in Fukui province has one from the late sixteenth century, on six panels, using as became customary the long oval shape to suggest a globe. Another attractive solution to the difficulties of flat projection—drawing the world in eleven sheets as if it were twenty-two slender long boats viewed from above—is in the manuscript map of 1759 by Sawada Kazunori, a many-pointed black fringe filling the spaces beyond his drawing.

Matteo Ricci's world map, published in China in 1600—part of the spread of learning—reached in Japan that half of the mind which desired literal rather than Buddhist truth. But there was never a Japanese work comparable with the great European atlases; nothing like the Ptolemaeus, Ortelius, Blaeu, Janssonius, which poured into the first two centuries of European printing their science transformed as works of art. Books on the history of map-making in Japan pass quickly from earlier centuries to the nineteenth, travelling through religious vision and among those who "instead of being cartographers in the true sense" produced "hybrids that lie between maps and Ukiyo-e style landscapes." A similar development marked changes in medical books, where the escape from a Confucian tradition to accurate anatomy came in a large work upon the Dutch model, the *Kaitai Shinsho* of Sugita Gempaku,[1] as late as 1774; and the first to show dissection from original Japanese observation was the *Kaitai Hatsumo* ("A New Work on Anatomy") published at Osaka in 1813. Needless to add that in Japanese hands even the less pleasing details of anatomy became color-woodblock works of art, but the date was late.

Nagakubo Sekisui, we learn, was "a Confucian scholar of Mito, and an accomplished geographer," living from 1707 to 1801. His world map, published in 1785 and often reprinted, was among a few before the nineteenth century which had influence; an oval world upon a large sheet measuring about 160 x 93 centimeters [Plate 92]. Hand-colored, on strong soft paper, this was printed from woodblocks. Early impressions, as in Shiba Kokan's more innovative world maps, used less color than was popular later. Asia, Africa, Europe, America give a fair impression

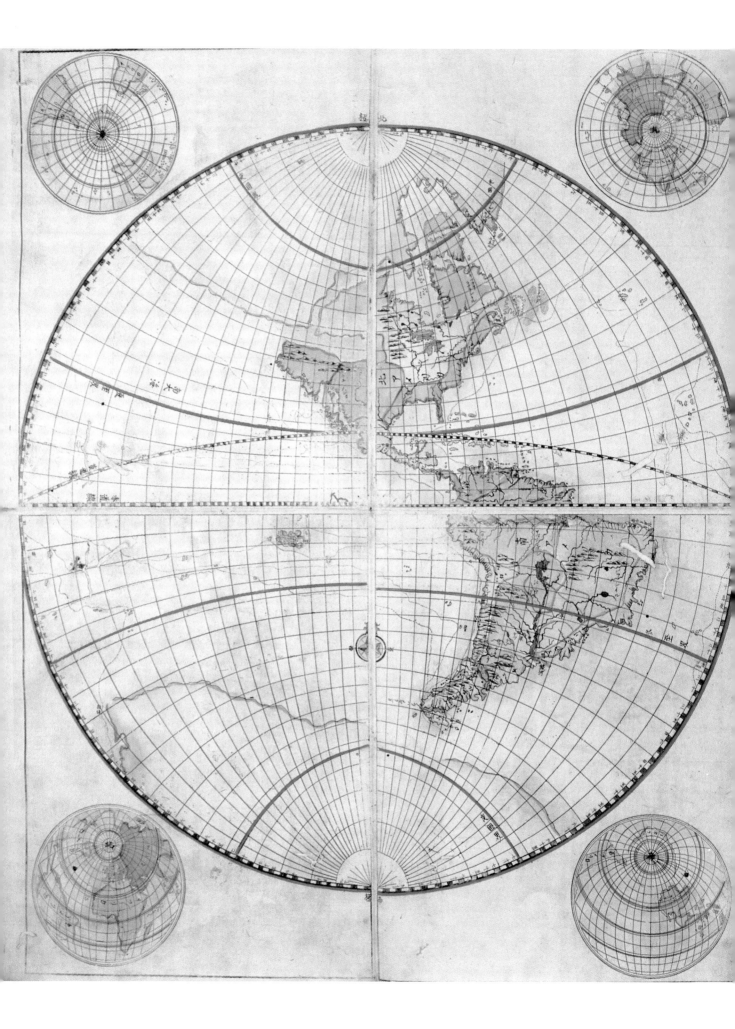

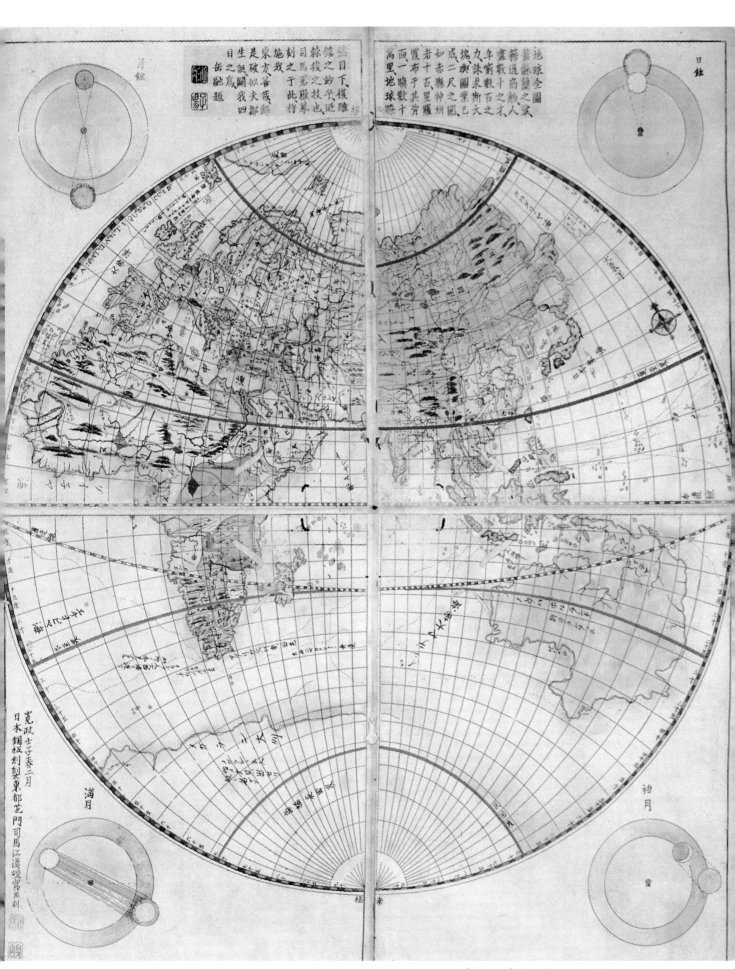

Plate 93. Shiba Kokan: World Map, 1792

of what we are accustomed to seeing, though in both these well-known maps South America leans far eastwards in the attempt to achieve a true global projection. Matsutaro expressed it very justly:

> Nagakubo's map appeared and continued to be widely used, revealing the extent to which Ricci's map influenced the world image of Japanese during the Edo period. On the other hand, the prevalence over such a long period of one map without major revisions reflects the influence of the feudal system and seclusion.

Shiba Kokan represented the escape from those confinements. His world map in two sheets, published in 1792, showed in the surrounding diagrams Copernican figures of the earth, sun and moon which his accompanying book explained with more diagrams [Plate 93]. Australia is present with an approximation of shape quite unknown to Nagakubo Sekisui; Brazil again stretches eastward in deformity, Japan is at the far east of a sheet, but this is a modern map. Ever original, Shiba Kokan describes himself in the colophon as introducing the technique of copper engraving to Japan; these two sheets are copper engravings, hand colored. Later impressions added considerably to the surrounding decoration, with little scenes of whaling, of hills and harbors and plant dissection; they were also more fully colored, in homage to Blaeu or popular taste. The spare early issue still conveys a sense of innovation. Shiba Kokan's maps are smaller, each sheet measuring about 54 x 45 centimeters.

The late arrival in Japan of scientific cartography, through a policy of isolation and absence of the urge to explore, produced historically a range of maps-as-art for which we may now feel truly grateful; yet dates are puzzling, for the pioneer in Japan who discovered how to measure degrees of latitude, Ino Tadataka, produced his results in the first fifteen years of the nineteenth century. Hokkaido in the north, an unexplored area for many centuries, called Ezo, was not known to be an island until mid-eighteenth century. The first reasonably true map of Hokkaido appeared in 1758, the work of Hayashi Shihei, and it landed him in prison.

As Japanese maps became merely accurate, one could expect them to be like any other modern maps, nothing much to write home about. Thus the space given to nineteenth-century developments, in books on the subject, is relatively uninteresting except for a surprise of early tradition surviving. Color woodblock printing, in the twenty-six folding maps of Tokyo from about 1820, gives great charm to that series. Areas of red, yellow, grey and blue define the rivers, streets, imperial estates, and shrines; domestic blocks within them give names of the land-owning families. There were and often are no street names in Japan, making particular addresses difficult to find. In totally changed Tokyo I have wondered whether taxi drivers still have these delightful maps in mind.

Tourist maps and subway plans keep something of an older style; efficient, of course, often inventive, clear in a spirit of enjoyable design, generally more fun than geometric diagrams prepared for any European network.

We arrive back almost at the point of departure. Awoki Szandow of Osaka, spelling his name thus, produced a color-printed folding map to go with his set of guide books "for Travellers Round the World." Flags adorn the top margin, a chart of mountains records their heights, a double-sided globe as in Shiba Kokan's world map is added. Shapes are copied faithfully, the nations colored with some disregard of convention. Pink, used generally for the British Empire, cannot have been well understood, for Awoki used it also for Japan, distinguished thus from the green mass of China. Printed by mixed method, the fine lines are engraved. A large wall map in my possession, from about the same time—1875, seventh year of Meiji— has national flags along all four borders and provides, in a wide area below, just such a series of relief-printed metal vignettes—thirty of them—as were found in the guide books: St. Peters in Rome, Nelson's Column, no native munched by crocodile but an empire-builder in his silk hat exploring street-markets in the Levant. The publisher was none other, of course, than Awoki Szandow of Osaka.

1. *New Book of Anatomy.* The Dutch work was *Ontleedkundige Tafelen*, 1734.

INDEX

Pages including illustrations are numbered in italics

Actor-prints, 74, 89, 94
Adams, William, 144
Albums, 31-32, 49, 50-51, 55, 57, 60, 67, 70, 72,
    74, 78, 80, 87-88, 90, 96, 98-99, 124
Amida, *11-12*, 19
Analects of Confucius, 20
Anatomy, 145
Antiquarian Booksellers' Association of Japan, 6
Aquatint, 51, 53, 63, 68
Asia Society, 32
Atlases, 145
Australia, 138, 148
Azuma No Teburi (Chinnen), 72, *73*, 81

Baitai, Ki, 70
Bakufu, 16, 18
Balloons, 135, 144
Bamboo, 50, 56, 58, 66-67, 75, 78, 81, 86, *98*
Beatty, Chester, 20, 25, 87
Bible, 14
Birds, 27, 51-52, 58, 70, 81, 86, 96, 126, 131
Blaeu, Johan 145, 148
Block-books, 15, 17, 102
Block-cutters, 15, 47, 54-55, 58-59, 63, 66, 91
Block-printing, 10, 25
Blockmakers, 59, 71, 74
Boats, 122-124, 129-131, 134, 145
Bodleian Library, 7

Bonkotsu, Igami, 128
Bookbinding, 33, 35, 60, 72
Books of Hours, 32-33
Booksellers, 4-6, 10, 26, 36, 38, 73
Bosai, Kameda, 80
Brazil, 148
Bridges, 116, 120-121, 123, 126, 129-130, 139
British Library, 7
British Museum, 10, 87, 89
Brocade, 19, 37-38, 43, 50
Brush-characters, 4
Buddhism, 3-6, 8-9, 11-14, 17-19, 21, 23, 27, 35,
    46, 141, 144
Bumpo, Kawamura, 47, 66, 71, 75, 78-79, 84
Bumpo Gafu, 78
Bun-sho Monogatari, 33, *34*
Buncho, 126
Bun'endo, 126-128
Burke, Jackson, 23
Burma, 139

California scroll, 41-42
Calligraphy, 3-4, 7-8, 14-15, 18, 24-26, 32-33,
    36-37, 39, 46, 49-50, 56-57, 59, 81-82, 85-88,
    90, 96
Caricature, 70, 72
Cartographers, 144-145
Cartography, 148
"Castaway" manuscript, 130-136, *132-133, 135*
Chibbett, David, 8n, 10-11, 22n

151

Chikudo, 80
China, 5-6, 18-20, 54-57, 139, 141, 145
Chinnen, Onishi, 72-73, 80-81
Chitsu, 47, 79
Christianity, 6, 46
Christmas cards, 87
Chromolithography, 51
Chushichi, Tanaka, 66
Color-printing, 31, 36, 55-57, 59, 61, 66, 72, 74-75, 84, 88, 90, 110
Confucius, 20, 145
Convenient Book for English (Suzando), 107-108, 136-137
Copernicus, 145, 148
Copper-plates, 128-129
Cortazzi, Sir Hugh, 144

Daihannya-kyo Sutra, 17
Daishi, Kobo, 12, 17, 19
Daishi, Dengyo, 19
De Hamel, Christopher, 25-26
Designers, 53-54, 59
Drawing, 58-59, 71, 84-85, 128
Drawings, 53, 70, 74, 85
Dress, 48, 98, 131, 139
Dutch, 102, 129-130, 144-145

Edinburgh, 138
Edo, 16, 66, 83, 122-124, 126
Edo Meisho Zue (Settan), 122-123, 124
Ehon Mushi-erabi (Utamaro), 94-95
Ehon Seiro Bijin Awase (Harunobu), 95
Ehon Yoroi Sakura, 62
Eigaku Kyoju, 105-106
Eigo Jizai, 107
Eishi, Hosoda, 91, 92-93
Emaki, 31-32, 38, 41, 46, 48, 51, 128
England, 6-7, 16, 51, 131, 139
Engraving, 10, 55, 68, 128-129, 136, 148
Ephemera, 87
Eskimos, 131, 138
Etching, 55, 68, 108, 129
Europe, 6-7, 14-17, 25, 31, 39, 46, 51, 54, 63, 68, 83, 89, 102, 106, 129, 137-139, 141, 144-145

Explorers, 131
Expressionism, 81

Facsimiles, 74, 84
Fan-makers, 112-113
Fans, 32, 58, 60, 84, 112-113, 144
Fashion, 25, 36, 58, 94, 117
Flowers, 63, 96
Fore-edges, 136
Forgery, 5, 26
Frogs, 81, 94-95
Frontispieces, 11, 13, 23, 27, 91, 96
Fruit, 33, 46, 75, 86, 94, 120
Fry, Roger, 70
Fugaku Hyakkei (Hokusai), 61, 96, 97-98
Fuji, Mount, 27, 50, 61, 84, 96-98, 129
Fujita, Tsukuji, 82
Fujiwara (clan), 9, 12, 18-19

Gafu (Suiseki), 72
Gampi, 3, 33
Geishas, 73, 95
Gempaku, Sugita, 145
Genji, Prince, 7
Genji Monogatari, 41
Genji, The Tale of, 7, 9, 17, 74, 75, 76-77
Geography, 128, 144
Gesso, Taniguchi, 85-86
Ginko, 60, 106-107
Gion Shrine, 47, 48-49
Goncourt, Edmond de, 12, 87, 89, 97
Goshun, Matsumura 80
Grammar, 102-103, 105
Great Japan Exhibition, 128
"Green Houses," 95
Guide-books, 109-140
Gyogi, 141-144

Haikai Hyaku Gasan (Gesso), 85-86
Haiku, 63, 71, 85-86
Hand-tinting, 35
Hanshin Meisho Zue, 126, 127, 128
Harunobu, 95
Hasshu Gafu, 55-59, 61, 63

Heian period, 9, 12, 17-18
Heibei, Tanaka, 66
Heike Monogatari, 18
Hidayoshi, Toyotomi, 16
Hieizan-ban, 3, 19
Hillier, Jack, 53, 67-68n, 74, 109, 126
Hiragana, 17, 19, 30, 36, 46
Hiroshige, Ando, 12
Hochu, Nakamura, 84
Hofer, Philip, 20
Hoitsu, Sakai, 82-83, 83-84
Hokkaido, 4, 148
Hokusai, Katsushika, 12, 61, 75, 84, 91, 96-98,
    126, 129, 144
Horyu-ji (temple), 5-6, 18, 25, 144
Hsuan-tsang, 13
Hundred Views of Fuji (Hokusai), 61, 96, 97-98
Hyakumanto Darani, 5-6, 6-7, 18, 26
Hyakumanto pagodas, 2, 4-8, 18
Hyde, Donald, 20, 22
Hyde, Mary, 21

I, Prince, 56
Ichiyu Gafu (Kuniyoshi), 94
Ieyasu, 16, 20, 27, 30, 125, 144
Illustrated Guide Book for Travellers Around Japan
    (Suzando), 136, 139-140
Illustrated Guide Book for Travellers Round the World
    (Suzando), 136-139
Illustrated London News, 137
Impressionism, 58, 63, 67
India, 139, 145
Inro, 144
Ippo, Mori, 126
Ise Monogatari, 27, 56
Ishida, Mosaku, 12
Isseido (bookshop), 26-27, 36
Iwaya Monogatari, 43

Janssonius, 145
Japanese-English Communication, 106
Japonisme, 12, 98, 128
Jesuits, 6, 16-17
Jihei, Inoue, 67

Jimbutsu Ryakuga-Shiki (Masayoshi), 84
Jingo-ji (temple), 23-24
Jingo-ji sutra, 24-25
Jodo Buddhism, 19-21
Johnson's Dictionary, 108
Jotoku-ji (temple), 145
Jusaburo, Tsutaya, 96

Kaei Tsugo, 102-103
Kafuku Nimpitsu (Kiho), 71
Kaido Kyoka Awase (Bumpo, Nangaku), 78
Kaishien Gaden, 55
Kaitai Hatsumo, 145
Kaitai Shinsho, 145
Kamakura, 11-12, 14, 18, 20, 22, 25, 42, 128
Kamchatka, 130
Kana, 9-10, 17
Kanda (district), 21
Kan'ei, Nishiyama, 82
Kanga Shinan Nihen (Bumpo), 78
Kanga Shinan Nihen (Kanyosai), 66, 78
Kanji, 9, 16, 20
Kano (school), 54, 61-62, 69, 125
Kanyosai, 63, 66, 78, 84
Kasuga (shrine), 18
Kasuga-ban, 18-19, 21, 25
Kasuga-ban Lotus Sutra, 21
Kawase, Dr., 26-27
Kazunori, Sawada, 145
Kegan Paul Bookshop, 89
Kegon (waterfall), 126
Keibun, 80
Keijo Gaen, 80
Keisai, 84-85, 144
Kencho-ji (temple), 20
Kenshi Gaen (Kanyosai), 63
Keyes, Roger, 85, 87
Kiho, Kawamura, 47, 71, 79-80
Kiho Gafu (Kiho), 79
Kitano-Tsuya Monogatari, 43, 44-45, 46
Kobe, 126
Koetsu, Hon'ami, 16, 62, 83
Kofuku-ji (temple), 13, 15, 18, 21, 63
Kofuku-ji scroll, 14-15

Kokan, Shiba, 10, 128-130, 134, 145, 147-149
Komyo, Empress, 8
Korea, 4, 10, 16, 35, 101, 141
Korin, 54, 62, 71, 83-84
Korin, Furutani, 98
Korin Gafu (Hochu), 84
Korin Gashiki (Minwa), 71, 84
Korin Hyakuzu (Hoitsu), 84
Koshu, Hatta, 79
Koshu Gafu (Koshu), 79
Koya-ban, 19
Koyasan, 9, 19, 22
Kraus, Hans P., 36
Kunisada I, 73-74, 75, 76-77
Kunisada II, 61
Kuniyoshi, 94
Kyochusan (Bosai), 80
Kyosai, Gyosai, 82-83
Kyosai Gaden (Kyosai), 82-83
Kyoto, 16, 18-19, 23-24, 36, 38-39, 48, 51-52, 67, 69, 71, 75, 78-80, 86-87, 110-112, 116, 117, 121-122, 126
Kyoto *Nara-ehon*, 39
Kyuro Gafu (Baitai), 70
Kyushu, 4

Levinson, Harry, 22
Lan T'ing Pavilion, 55
Line-block, 63
Line-drawing, 61, 67
Lithography, 10, 55, 85, 102
London, 89, 117, 125, 128, 137

Mahayana Buddhism, 18-19
Mainz, 14
Maki, 7
Maki-mono, 4
Malay Peninsula, 139
Manga (Hokusai), 84, 97
Manga Hyaku-jo (Minwa), 71
Manuscripts, 7, 10, 25, 33, 36, 53
Maps, 128, 139, 141-145
Marbling, 108, 136
Maruyama (school), 54, 67

Masayoshi, Kitao, 81, 84-85
Matsutaro, 148
Medical books, 145
Meiji (era), 6, 17-18, 59, 82, 84, 98, 101-102, 131, 149
Meiji, Emperor, 6, 101
Meika Gafu, 80
Meisho-zue, 109-141, 110-112, 114-125, 127
Metal-cut, 136
Mezzotint, 63, 68
Mica, 16, 20, 62, 79, 85, 88, 94, 131
Millais, J.E., 66
Minamoto (clan), 18, 42
Ming Dynasty, 57
Miniatures, 32, 38
Minko, Tachibana, 86
Minwa, Aikawa, 71
Missionaries, 139, 145
Mitchell, C.H., 68n, 126
Miyako Meisho Zue (Shunchosai), 110-121, 110-112, 114-121
MOA Bijutsukan, 41
Mokyo Wakan Zatsuga (Kanyosai), 63, 64-65, 66
Momoyogusa (Sekka), 99-100
Morikuni, Tachibana, 62-63
Moronobu, 61-62
Morris, William, 13, 50, 73, 111
Moscow, 130-131, 134
Movable type, 10, 15-17, 101-102
Murasaki, Lady, 9, 17
Murase, Miyeko, 32
Music, 39, 72, 82, 121
Musicians, 86, 135, 139
Mustard Seed Garden, The, 56, 58, 59-61

Nagasaki, 66, 129
Nanga (school), 54, 61, 66, 80-81, 86, 94, 125
Nangaku, 78
Nantei, Nishimura, 72
Nantei Gafu (Nantei), 72
Nara, 5-6, 8-9, 18, 23, 25, 31-32, 48, 142
Nara-ehon, 31-33, 36-39, 43, 49, 144
Nara-period scroll, 26
New York Public Library, 20

Nikko, 27, 30, 125-126, 128
Nikko San Shi, 125-126
Nikko sutra, 27
Nishikizuri onna sanjurokkasen, 90, 91, 92-93
Noh, 16, 27, 30, 62
Noh manuscript, 28-29

Okyo, 67
Ortelius, A., 145
Osaka, 72, 82, 107, 126, 136, 138, 145, 149
Oson Gafu (Hoitsu), 82-83

Pagodas, 5-6, 8, 12, 18, 22, 26
Painters, 51, 58-60, 83, 86
Papermaking, 3, 5, 8
Papers, 4, 7-8, 11, 14, 25, 27, 49, 56, 62, 84
Parchment, 7
Pekarik, Andrew, 90
Photography, 10, 139, 144
Phrase-books, 101-108, 136
Poetry, 27, 50, 59, 85
Portuguese, 16, 144
Priests, 4, 7, 17, 23, 27, 32, 39, 58, 70, 72, 126
Printers, 14, 58, 61, 82, 110, 126
Printsellers, 124
Ptolemaeus, C., 145
Publishers, 56, 59, 101, 125, 136
Punch-cutters, 15
Pure Land Buddhism, 19-21

Ransai Gafu (Ransai), 66-67
Ransai, Mori, 58, 66
Realism, 69-71, 78, 125-126
Redouté, P. J., 51
Relief-metal printing, 139, 149
Ricci, Matteo, 145
Rice, 8, 10, 72, 79-80, 111, 124
Rimpa (school), 54, 62, 83-84, 94, 98-99
Roberts, Laurence, 122
Romanticism, 69
Running-hand, 90
Ryerson Collection, 33, 35
Ryotai, 63
Ryuko Meibutsushi (Soan), 86

Sado Island, 48
Saga (province), 16, 55-56
Saga-bon, 16, 30, 32, 39, 55-57, 83
Saiga Shokunin Burui (Minko), 86
Sake, 56, 78, 95, 98, 105, 111, 113, 124
Samurai, 72, 94, 113
Sanskrit, 25
Sansom, Sir George, 9, 15
Sansui Gafu (Bumpo), 78
Sansui Ryakuga-Shiki (Masayoshi), 84-85
Screen-painting, 95-96
Screens, 35, 39, 48-49, 84, 86, 95, 113, 134, 145
Script, 9, 19, 30, 102, 105
Scrolls, 4, 7-8, 23, 25-26, 30-31, 33, 42-43, 47, 48, 56-57, 101
Scroll-mounts, 19
Sculpture, 6, 9, 12
Seiro Bijin Awase Sugata Kagami (Shigemasa, Shunso), 95-96
Seiro Ehon Nenju-gyoji (Utamaro), 95
Seitei, Watanabe, 82
Seiyu Ryotan (Kokan), 129
Sekigahara, Battle of, 30
Sekisui, Nagakubo, 142-143, 145, 148
Sekka, Kamisaka, 99-100
Seo, Audrey Yoshiko, 99
Seso Hyakushi (Toshu), 74
Sessai, Masuyama, 52
Settan, Hasegawa, 110, 122
Settei, 62
Shakespeare, 50, 60
Sharaku, 12, 74, 94
Shigemasa, Kitao, 95
Shihei, Hayashi, 148
Shijo (school), 52, 54, 69-71, 74-75, 79-80, 87, 88, 94, 109-110, 125
Shijo *surimono*, 87, 88
Shikoku, 4, 6
Shimizu, Yutaka, 8n, 31, 33, 43
Shingon Buddhism, 17
Shinto, 13, 18, 35, 50, 117
Shonin, Honen, 19
Shoso-in, 25, 101, 143
Shotoku, Empress, 5, 8

Shotoku-Taishi Nara-ehon, 36-38
Shrines, 30, 32, 38, 123-125, 129, 139, 148
Shunchosai, Takehara, 110
Shunga, 94-95
Shunsho, Katsukawa, 95-96
Silk, 4, 19, 38, 46-47, 49-52, 74
Silk-screen, 98
Sketchbooks, 67, 97, 128
So Shiseki Gafu (Ransai), 66
Soan, Sakuma, 86
Soan, Suminokura, 16, 62, 83
Soken, Yamaguchi, 61, 66-68, 70-71, 80
Soken Gafu (Soken), 67
Soken Sansui Gafu (Soken), 67-68
Sonan Gafu (Chinnen), 81-82
Sorimachi, Shigeo, 21-22, 27, 32, 36-38, 43, 46
Soyaku, Eikaiwa, 104
Stone-engraving, 57
Suiboku, 67
Suiseki, Sato, 72
Sumi, 57, 63, 68, 80
Suntory Museum, 41
Surimono, 86, 87-88
Sutras, 5, 7-9, 11, 17-18, 21-27, 33
Suzando [Szandow], Aoki, 107, 136, 149

Tadataka, Ino, 148
Taiga, Ikeno [Taigado], 58, 80-81
Taigado Gafo (Taiga), 80
Taira (clan), 18, 42
Taisho (period), 74
Taiwan, 49
Taizan, 74
Tale of Genji, The, 7, 9, 17, 74, 75, 76-77
Tanroku, 35, 39
Tatebe, Mokyo, 63
Tea, 57, 63, 72, 95, 108, 113, 117, 122, 126
Teito Gakei Ichiran (Bumpo), 78
Temples, 5-9, 11, 17-18, 20, 22, 38, 139
Ten Ox-Herding Pictures, 14
Tendai Buddhism, 3, 19, 21
Thirty-six Immortal Women Poets, 90, 91, 92-93
Todai-ji (temple), 8, 18
Tokaido Road, 12

Tokugawa (period), 14, 16-18, 20, 30, 33, 72, 110, 122, 128
Tokyo, 81, 110, 122-124, 148
Tokyo National Museum, 4, 18, 27, 41
Torinoko, 3, 33, 35, 37, 43
Tosa (school), 14, 33, 35, 54, 144
Toshu, Tamate, 74
Toyo, 80
Toyokuni III [Kunisada I], 73, 89, 99
Toyoshiko, 80
Travel, 6, 55, 109, 128, 130, 136, 141
Tripitaka, 23

Ukiyo-e, 67, 69, 71, 73-75, 87, 89-91, 94-95, 109, 111, 125, 129, 145
Umpitsu Soga (Morikuni), 62, 63
Utamaro, Kitagawa, 12, 39, 63, 94-95, 96, 110

Virgin, Louise, 88

Waei Tsugo, 106
Waley, Arthur, 10
Water-color, 74, 131
Waterfalls, 24, 88, 125-126, 139
Whaling, 129, 148
Women, 8, 71, 81, 84, 90-91, 95, 124
Woodblock, 5, 10, 13, 15, 31, 47, 55-57, 63, 74, 85, 88, 91, 129, 148
Woodcut, 10-15, 19, 35, 53, 57, 62-63, 67-68, 84-88, 98, 102, 111, 116, 122-123, 126, 129
World Map (Kokan), 146-147, 148
World Map (Sekisui), 142-143, 145, 148

Yamato Jimbutsu Gafu (Soken), 70
Yamato-e, 54, 111, 144
Yoshiakira, Hanagata, 91
Yoshiwara (district), 95
Yuzu-nembutsu-engi, 14

Zen Buddhism, 17, 19-20, 35, 50, 54, 61, 67, 69, 100
Zumwinkle, Richard, 8n, 39n

This colophon is from the original fine press printing.

THIS book was designed by Jonathan Clark at The Artichoke Press in Mountain View, California. The text is set in Scripps College Old Style, originally designed by Frederic W. Goudy between 1939 and 1947; this digital version was produced by Sumner Stone and is used by courtesy of Scripps College. The display face is Charlemagne, an Adobe type designed by Carol Twombly, who also drew the special version used on the title page. Decorations throughout the book are taken from traditional Japanese patterns. Scanning and lithography by Shoreline Printing, Mountain View. Bindings and slipcases made by Roswell Bookbinding, Phoenix. Four hundred and fifty copies were printed for members of The Book Club of California, San Francisco: May–October 1999.